JEFF STELLING

I've Got Mail

The *Soccer Saturday* Letters

HEADLINE

First published in 2020 by
HEADLINE PUBLISHING GROUP

First published in paperback in 2021 by
HEADLINE PUBLISHING GROUP

1

Cataloguing in Publication Data is available from the British Library

ISBN 978 1 4722 7978 1

Designed and typeset by EM&EN
Printed and bound in Great Britain by Clays Ltd, Elcograf S.p.A.

Headline's policy is to use papers that are natural, renewable and recyclable
products and made from wood grown in well-managed forests and other
controlled sources. The logging and manufacturing processes are expected
to conform to the environmental regulations of the country of origin.

HEADLINE PUBLISHING GROUP
An Hachette UK Company
Carmelite House
50 Victoria Embankment
London EC4Y 0DZ

www.headline.co.uk
www.hachette.co.uk

Dear Lizzie, Robbie, Matt and Olivia,

Thank you for your forbearance as I wrote this, crashing away noisily at the keyboard on the family PC with the same force that I used when I was hammering furiously at the keys on the 1970s Olivetti typewriter at the start of my career.

This one is for you.

All my love.

Jeff

Contents

Author's Note

Some of the names of correspondents quoted in this book have been changed to preserve their anonymity.

The original spelling, punctuation and grammar have been retained in all the correspondence reproduced in this book, except for a few words in which letters have been replaced by asterisks.

PREFACE

It arrived while I was playing football. I remember my
mum running towards me, dressed in pinny and slip-
pers, waving a piece of flesh-coloured paper gripped in
her hand, the print all in slightly faded block capitals.
But the message from my new employer was clear and
urgent:

BERNARD GENT UNWELL. GO TO LEEDS IMMEDIATELY.
COVER LEEDS UNITED V MIDDLESBROUGH.

It was the first and last telegram I ever received. They
were already near obsolete by the late 1970s and would
be removed from service four years later. But my family
did not own a telephone at the time so this was the
quickest way of making contact. I did what I was told
and went to Leeds immediately – or at least as soon
as I could persuade my girlfriend to drive me there as

I didn't own a car, nor had I passed my test. I also hoped that it was downhill most of the way from Teesside to Leeds as the ageing off-white NSU 500 (an exaggeration as the engine size is 479 cc) in which we would be travelling had an aversion to going uphill. I had ended up pushing the thing plenty of times after summer Sunday jaunts from Hartlepool to Durham. It had an alleged top speed of 59 mph, but that was clearly only with a strong following wind or else in the manufacturer's wildest imagination. We rarely managed to top 40 mph. Still, I was grateful for it now.

It was a message that probably changed the course of my life. Bernard Gent was the long-standing, well-respected reporter on Middlesbrough games for Radio Tees and I had only joined the station a week earlier as a news reporter. It was my first radio job and I had never been on air. Here I was thrust into live broadcasting of a top-flight football match, which was also regarded as a local derby, played at a hell for leather pace in front of a loud, vibrant Elland Road crowd. I had never been to Leeds, let alone the football ground. I didn't know where to collect my ticket for the game or, when I was inside, how to send my updates (mobile phones were still years away). Thankfully, some grizzled local newspaper reporters whose kindness I will never forget helped me out. Somehow, I managed to send a series of at least semi-coherent match reports back to listeners on Teesside.

Forty-eight hours later, at the start of my second week at the station, at the age of 22, I was asked to switch to sports reporting and my future was changed inexorably.

It was the first of many pieces of correspondence during my life which have made me laugh, cry or perhaps influenced my pathway in a more significant way.

In 1977, receiving a telegram was the ultimate in excitement. I knew as my mum overlapped our full-back to deliver it, that it must contain something significant. And it did. Having lived through a world war, mum was alarmed, because in her mind telegrams only contained bad news. Thankfully, this one didn't.

But getting letters either by post or these days in the form of e-mail has always been important. Even now I feel slightly disappointed if the postman passes the door without anything for me even though I know the chances are it will be a bill, a parking fine, a bank statement (memo to self: online banking) or a catalogue offering me clothing or garden furniture. The same applies when my in-box is empty save for someone offering a deal on a used car or urging me to change my energy provider.

So the following represents a cross-section of correspondence sent to me down the years, both the good and the bad. They are all here, warts and all. Including those liberally sprinkled with spelling, shall we say, inconsistencies and grammatical gremlins – even though I had to asterisk some of the swear words for our more sensitive readers.

These days my mail is often from total strangers, usually with a simple birthday or autograph request. But at times they are emotional and sometimes angry. Occasionally, they entrust me with personal issues that they probably would not tell their closest friends. The only thing they all have in common is they all start, 'Dear Jeff'. Or almost all do . . .

1

HATE MAIL

Jeff Stelling – Shit.

That was all it said on the envelope. Just the three words. No address. No stamp. But credit to the Royal Mail, it ended up on my desk as quickly as if it had been posted first class. It was all the more impressive as I had only been at LBC/IRN, London's rolling news station, for around four months.

Like most journalists, it had always been my ambition to work in Fleet Street and this was as near as it got in broadcasting terms, our studios tucked away in Gough Square, separated from the most historic and famous newspaper street in the world by only the width of the Cheshire Cheese, an almost equally historic and famous pub – the perfect watering hole at the end of a hard day, once the droves of tourists had headed for their hotels or evening meals.

But the truth is, it had not been an easy transition.

I was working in the Northeast as head of my own sports department and had a regular sport and music show. We covered all the region's football clubs from Sunderland in the north to York in the south, including my beloved Hartlepool. In truth though my favourite club to visit in those days was York City, managed by former Bolton goalkeeper Charlie Wright. I would arrive at around 10 am to be welcomed with a drink. Not tea or coffee, but Newcastle Brown Ale from a crate that Charlie kept by his desk. It seemed compulsory to have at least a couple. It may have helped put the manager at ease. It helped put me to sleep.

I had initially turned down a job at LBC/IRN on the basis that my wife and I were buying a new home in the Northeast overlooking a golf course and with upstairs and downstairs toilets. To a council house boy from Hartlepool, the two-toilet home was an impossible dream, life was good and so we decided to stay put.

But we never got to flush either toilet. Four months later, the job came up again and this time we decided to take a chance. A few weeks later, after a fortnight in a seedy Bayswater hotel, we found ourselves living in a ground-floor flat on the North End Road in Fulham, sharing a toilet and a kitchen with another flat. The TV operated on 50 pence pieces, there was a tin shower in the corner of the bedroom and a group of punk rock-ers lived on the floor above. My wife used to send me upstairs to tell them to keep the noise down at one or two in the morning. Strangely, they could never hear my knock! It was the long hot summer of 1981, when London was in the grip of riots, so rather than look out over the 18th green as we would have done, our view was of bus-loads of policemen clasping shields and batons, waiting to be called into action. Feeling vulnerable, I would often stand behind the front door armed with the only weapon available to me, usually a half-empty whisky bottle, in case anyone broke through police lines. The bottle was never half-empty by the end of the night.

Soon after we upgraded to a one-bedroomed flat above the local greengrocer with close-up views of the overground section of the District Line, with the first train rattling loudly past at around 5.30 every morning apart from Sunday when we could lie in undisturbed until 6.13.

Things were not going much better at my office. My boss, Mike Lewis had received a letter of complaint within the first couple of weeks. 'For god's sake, get the bloke with the Geordie accent off. We can't understand a word he says,' was the gist.

Mike wrote back, 'I am sure in this day and age you would agree regional accents are to be encouraged.'

But our correspondent was determined to have the last word. 'Regional accents are to be encouraged. But speech defects are not!'

I hated everything about the job and the city so much that I started applying for jobs at regional radio stations. I was especially keen on a position at Radio West in Bristol. Having got the job at LBC/IRN, I felt confident I would be successful. Too confident. I got an interview but not the job. For the first (and last) time ever, I rang the station to ask the Programme Controller why I had not been chosen.

'To be honest,' he said, 'I didn't really like you.'

Well, I did ask.

And then there was the letter: *Jeff Stelling – Shit.*

How dare a simple git like you speak unkindly about John McEnroe, a genious [sic]. Are you good at anything? As a matter of fact we have been wanting to write about your horrible accent. The same as that lunatic on the darts programme (Sid Waddell) when the lovely Mr Bristow is on. You and him and Paisley have the most horrible accents. So why don't you stick your head in shit rather than speak unkindly about the best tennis player in the world. You are so simple, you talk about fucking football as if it was a matter of life or death. How dare you speak about anyone Irish

American when you are so useless. So go and put your head in the lavatory pan or go on a trip in a barrel down Niagara Falls, you simple shit. When we hear your horrible weak voice we usually turn you off. If you were as good as one of John McEnroe's toes you would be something. John McEnroe would think it an insult to be on the same programme as you, you shit. Watch what you say about anyone Irish in future, you shit.

The final 'you shit' was double underlined to make sure I got the message.

The reason for the outburst was a weekly and, I thought, good humoured, pithy if occasionally acerbic and opinionated review of the week's sporting press. A colleague had done something similar for years at Radio Tees in the Northeast without complaint. After a handful of weeks, I had managed to incur the wrath of an Irishman, not advisable in that era. I was determined to leave London. And I did. Nineteen years later.

Many jobs and many years after the letter, I found myself presenting *Soccer Saturday* on Sky Sports. As the programme established itself, the volume of post increased but I was protected from abuse, or so it seemed, by an unlikely guardian angel, Rodney Marsh. He had the monopoly when it came to complaints. There was one stage when Rodney individually would receive more complaints than the rest of Sky TV put together. Job well done, I thought. He was on the panel to provoke argument and discussion and win the fledgling show a few headlines – and he was a master of his craft. Personally, I was very sorry when he lost his job over his 'Toon Army'/Tsunami gag on the phone-in show, *You're On Sky Sports*. He and the station hoped that if he kept a low profile for a while, he might one day be able to return. But low profile and Rodney are not natural bedfellows and he never came back. I still speak to him occasionally as a guest on a radio show he co-hosts in America, aptly entitled *Grumpy Pundits*.

When Rodney departed, my hate mail increased. At times people have used public platforms to criticise *Soccer Saturday*, no-one with more vitriol than journalist Jonathan Liew in the *Daily Telegraph* who wrote: 'I really hope you have sufficient joy, taste and loving people in your life to be able to fill your Saturday afternoon more productively than by sluicing its chortling, barrel-scraping, cod-football sewage into your eyes.' Not a fan then.

But it was a column in the *Sun* that produced one of the most vitriolic pieces of correspondence. In fact, a column is an exaggeration. I simply used to predict Premier League results in each Saturday's paper. What could be offensive about that? Of course these days it is easy to abuse someone using Twitter and 140 characters. But to find some paper and an envelope, buy a stamp, discover the correct address, write the letter and then go and post the thing, you really have to hate someone. And this fella did:

Dear Jeff Stelling,

Big Neil Solomon here on the pen. Listen here you podgy, grinning, stupid, slimey, big headed twat. You old codger, clueless c*** of a man. You stupid Stelling with the worst possible Saturday football predictions. You always get most wrong, you fucking joke, Stelling. I support Fulham yet you always slag 'em. You always predict them to lose. Stelling says it's Liverpool 2 Fulham 0, you c***. If you slag Fulham off once more then I am going to smash your face (we would not even notice you podgy p****!!) You best predict next time I read in Sun Goals that it's Fulham 3 Liverpool 0.

I dashed to that Saturday's edition of the *Sun* and there it was in black and white, Fulham 0 Liverpool 3. Oh no . . .

Actually Big Neil had found some paper but not writing paper. He had written this on the back of his mobile phone bill. But he had cunningly concealed his details by sellotaping a piece of paper across that part of his bill. Equally cunningly, I peeled the Sellotape off. On the back of the piece of paper that he had used to hide those details, was the prescription for the medication he was taking at the time of writing!

So Big Neil, if you are reading this – Come on Fulham!

2

LOVE LETTERS

Thankfully, the great majority of letters to *Soccer Saturday* have been more conventional fan mail.

In its earliest days, the show was often described in the press as having a cult following. I was never sure whether this was a compliment or not. I always felt a cult was something that was followed devotedly by not very many people. So letters were a good guide to how we were doing. Of course, some were more enthusiastic than others.

Dear Jeff,

Before I start you do an amazing job on Gillette Soccer Saturday, like a conductor in an orchestra. Sheer perfection!

I am writing on behalf of my wife, Samantha. I suppose everyone says they are your biggest fan, but I reckon my wife is right up there. She is not freaky or stalkerish or anything weird (well, I hope not). She is known at work as the Jeff Stelling fan as she has two signed photos of you on her desk, one from Sky Sports, one from Countdown. I got them from an autograph seller and they take pride of place on her desk. It gets some serious respect from the blokes in the office.

We are coming to your show in May and I would like to ask if there is a chance she could get a photo with you before or after the event to add to her collection on the desk at work?

She never misses Soccer Saturday and when she has to work she even Sky+'s it!'

I never actually did the show in question for reasons that we will discuss later in the book, but I think it is safe to say Samantha is my No 1 fan!

Pretty much every week we receive requests for birthdays and weddings – and once even for a funeral. I can't remember the exact details but I do remember Merse, Tiss, Charlie, Thommo and me solemnly doing pieces to camera to be shown at the wake along the lines of, 'We are so sorry Bill isn't watching us today . . .'

Most of the wedding requests are pretty straightforward and the panel usually record witty 'Don't do it James/Olly/Nick' messages but some are more specific:

Jeff, my name is Bella and I am getting married next year. My future husband to be (Matthew – who I call Lionbear haha) thinks you are amazing and I am sending this message to ask a big favour please. I am involved in a group where we exchange love notes all around the world with different locations and I am asking if you could do one for my husband to be? It would involve you recording a message, and then sending me the photo. This is the message:

> Mr Lionbear
> My Love for You is so big it has reached
> Me – Jeff Sterling [sic] at Sky Sports
> Happy Wedding Day

Do you think you could do this? It would be amazing if you could and I know it would make his day (though being married to me should be enough really haha. My e mail address is tinkerbella1234@sky.com.

I tried, I really did. But with the boys watching I just couldn't get past Mr Lionbear without corpsing. Bella, or to be more formal, Tinkerbella, never did get her wedding message.

It is always especially satisfying to get letters from people within the game. The ever lovely Delia Smith at Norwich wrote to me some years ago:

Dear Jeff,

I have been meaning to write for ages as I simply adore the programme. How is it that I can sit down at 12 noon, stay there until 4.50 pm by which time I am on the very edge of my seat with excitement having watched no football at all?

Thanks for all the lovely programmes.

With warm wishes,

Delia

Delia and I have kept in touch and become friends. So much so that when I asked her to be the Dictionary Corner guest on *Countdown* she was happy to help, as long as she could get from her home in East Anglia to Manchester and back in the same day. But with recording days starting early and finishing late, this was proving difficult. It wasn't until after the five shows were finished that production staff told me that Delia had solved this particular conundrum herself, by hiring a private plane and paying for it herself.

I also still treasure a letter written in 2010 from the late Doug Ellis, who as well as praising *Soccer Saturday*, had some thoughts on another series of shows I was present-ing called *Time of Our Lives* which brought together three guests to reflect on great footballing teams or events with which they had been involved. It was a lovely series to do with great characters telling wonderful stories. I remember one bringing together Manchester City greats Franny Lee, Mike Summerbee and Joe Corrigan where they told how the team would put on a Christmas panto every year at the City Supporters' Club. Big Joe had been Widow Twanky in the most recent one. You could not imagine it these days! And another where Peter Shilton revealed he had been training for a European Cup final with his goalkeeping coach in the centre of a traffic island on the instructions of the Nottingham Forest manager Brian Clough. Doug had enjoyed it:

Dear Jeff,

As the old man of professional football (director and chairman at Villa for 35 years), I am writing to congratulate you on all your programmes but particularly your latest 'Time Of Our Lives' when you interviewed so many old friends of mine who mentioned the likes of Matt Busby, Bill Shankly, Don Revie, Bill Nicholson, Stan Cullis, Ron Atkinson, Dave Bassett etc. I have been fortunate to know all of these men and it all brought back so many happy memories (In fact I interviewed both Don Revie and Dave Bassett for the managership of Villa.)

Since selling the club to Randy Lerner, I am now President but when I am not watching Villa, I can be found watching Sky Sports. Your enthusiasm and humour is infectious. Long may it continue.

With kindest regards,

Doug Ellis

Don Revie, manager of Aston Villa?! Now that would have been some story, a real headline-maker.

And it was because of making headlines that I got a lovely letter from Richard Scudamore, Chief Executive of the Premier League after I had helped launch a new Premier League season. I was one of a clutch of Sky Sports presenters doing live inserts into *Sky Sports News* to promote a new season.

They all went smoothly. Except for one. Mine. I had arrived a little late at the venue and had no real chance to rehearse, but it was straightforward enough. All I had to do was a live interview with five footballing figures, managers, players and referee Mike Dean, on a raised stage. All went well until I got to the final interviewee, last in a line stretched across the stage, Hull City's captain Ian Ashbee. To make sure I wasn't blocking him from view of the camera, I moved an extra step to the right, not realising the stage didn't extend an extra step to the right. I went careering off the stage, crashing three feet to the floor, notes flying everywhere, pride and posterior both hurt. I appealed to Mike Dean that I must have been tripped, but of course he had not seen it. But it ensured front and back-page headlines the following day in the national press for the Premier League launch. Richard wrote congratulating me for ensuring this launch got more column inches than any other ever had.

If I have one regret over my career, it is occasionally that I am not doing something more worthwhile for society. Perhaps being a doctor, a teacher or a police-man. An air raid warden. The truth is though that I can't really cope with the sight of blood, I am not bright enough to teach and I wasn't tall enough to be a copper (in the days when there were height restrictions). And despite what Thommo would have you believe, I wasn't born during World War II. My dad, who was a shift worker in the local Hartlepool steelworks, always said, 'Do whatever you like son as long as you don't work at the bloody steelworks.'

But one letter that I received made me think that perhaps the job I do *is* worthwhile. I can say without any question, it is the single most moving letter I have received in my 47 years in journalism and broadcasting. It was written by someone who simply signed herself Anne Marie:

Dear Jeff Stelling,
   Gosh this is a difficult letter to start. I know the

middle and I know the ending but I haven't given the beginning much consideration. I guess this is a letter of thanks and gratitude for something which you will have no knowledge of even contributing to. But I am going to enlighten you. So just indulge me for a bit.

Ten years ago represents the darkest period of my life. I was 15 years old and clinically depressed. Yes, diagnostically confirmed at fifteen. It wasn't for the want of a loving home network and I wasn't a victim of an incessant school bullying campaign. I was just depressed. Plain and simple. Horrendously suffocating in a morbid black hole with seemingly no escape. A truly gut wrenching feeling to be perfectly frank. My GP's solution – medication. And rightly or wrongly I succumbed to the train of thought that a pill would make it all better. But it didn't. And I was finding it increasingly difficult to locate the escape route. I stumbled and rallied but couldn't quite jump out of that wretched black hole.

The one Saturday my brother was aimlessly channel flicking in that annoying sibling manner that only he can muster and I was entrapped in a particularly disconsolate case of the blues. He switched on Sky Sports News and hence Soccer Saturday because the suspense of not knowing the Chelsea score was gnawing away at him (if memory serves me correctly they were 2–0 up at Bolton). While staring at the screen (as you raved enthusiastically about whoever was top scorer in the PL at that particular time) a ghoulish thought crossed my mind: 'I'd be doing well to still be alive watching this, this time next week.' What macabre thinking! Nevertheless what ensued was a bizarre battle with my subconscious. All week, the only thing that kept me functioning was 'Get to Saturday'.

I teased and coaxed my subconscious. 'Come on, just stick it out for one more day.' And hallelujah, somewhat miraculously, I got to Saturday. And seeing your face was something of a mini-victory. Me 1 Depression 0. And so this sort of game was established. This preposterous two player game, which encompassed me battling my subconscious and which persevered for weeks upon weeks. 'Just get to Saturday,' became the mantra. Your face became the arbiter between victory and failure. And once those victories accumulated, the enjoyment I used to get out of life, slowly trickled back with them. And the weekly gulf in points tally between me and my dreaded foe became so great that depression was eventually relegated into oblivion.

Now I know all this sounds very ridiculous. But that's what depression is. Ridiculous. It's ridiculous and narcissistic and blooming relentless. But I got through it. Ten years later I'm still here and pleased to report that the dark days are confined to the past. And in a meandering sort of way, it's thanks to you. And so I just wanted to take this opportunity to say quite simply – Thank You. Thank you for the random statistics, the truly god awful puns, the colleague weight/height/physique jousting, the Hartlepool high jinks, the weekly deceptive dance of one team has scored only for it to transpire that the exact opposite has materialized and the rattling off of scores at warp speed with no consideration for carbon dioxide to oxygen rations as 5 pm edges ever closer. Thank you for all the aforementioned which distracted my mind long enough so I could clamber out of that god-forsaken black hole undetected.

Yours sincerely,

Anne Marie

I am not ashamed to say I wept when I read of Anne Marie's struggle. It's a letter I keep to this day. I am so pleased I could help her even if it was unwittingly. And she helped me unwittingly too, to understand people's mental struggles and to understand that actually my job does have value. I still though don't know what she meant by 'god awful puns' . . .

3

DREAM TEAM

Occasionally people ask what my dream *Soccer Saturday* panel would be. I tell them I have spent years sitting alongside my dream panels. Of course not everyone agrees!

Dear Jeff,

As a fellow Scotsman and a Celtic supporter, I have always been an admirer of the playing abilities of former players like the toothless Charlie 'Sit-u-ae-shun' Nicholas and Alan 'No teeth, always scratching his big nose, slobbering' McInally (he looks even worse in that scruffy beard). Unfortunately, they are much less proficient as television presenters. Where they fall short is in their less than clear and, at times, incomprehensible and uncompromising way of enunciating to a predominantly English television audience. They sound like they are talking to some

Scottish geezer outside a pub in Glasgow after having a few drinks. I don't expect them to deliver their lines like Alec Guinness or Laurence Olivier, but there must surely be a limit? Their diction leaves a lot to be desired to say the least. 'How now brown cow!' The rain in Spain stays mainly in the plain!' I am not a fan of the very unappealing, slimey and creepy looking Gary Lineker but he did at least have some elocution lessons before he became a BBC sports presenter. These two stooges should do the same. He even learned to speak Spanish when he played for Barcelona. These two can hardly speak English properly.

This was a proper rant. Some folk would say our correspondent's 'bum was out the windae'. They would be safe to do so, as judging from his comments he would not understand what the heck they were talking about anyway. But he wasn't finished. There were targets other than Nicholas, McInally and Lineker (not a bad front three by the way):

Whoever thought they would make ideal television sports presenters must, in the footballers' vernacular, be 'having a laugh'. They are certainly over-indulged just like their cricketing counterparts, Ian 'Beefy, nothing to say, elephant in the room' Botham, Michael 'totally incomprehensible' Holding, and the completely uncharismatic Mike Atherton with his totally crap, flat voice. Atherton has very much ridiculously long outstayed his welcome!

That's football and cricket done. Or so I thought.

The slobby, gormless Paul Merson is another elephant in the room as he doesn't even know the difference between Dundee and Dundee United. Why do you have these shallow charlatans on the show anyway?

As a result (no pun intended) I can't watch Sky Sports News any longer and have now switched over to BBC's final score. Chris Sutton, another ex-Celt has now moved to BT Sport and is much more articulate and a better speaker anyway.

A former viewer

Phew. Thank goodness that was over. But hang on . . .

PS The saddest and most depressing part is that football and sport in general is taking over the world and that is definitely not a good thing. If you don't like football with its never-ending season, unnecessary play-offs, pointless friendlies, marathon tournaments, moronic, inane chatter by pundits and crass, yobbish adverts for beer and betting, you might as well be dead or a football widow! R.I.P.

I am not convinced the writer really is a Celtic fan, to be truthful.

The only time I ever have problems understanding Charlie is when he says it's my round.

Charlie is a fan of Arsenal, Celtic, midfield runners and a deep thinker. Every week he is guaranteed to start at least one sentence with, 'I'm sitting here thinking'. We want our panel to get excited of course during the match they are watching at 3 o'clock. Charlie is a world leader in this. Time and again I have crossed to him excitedly after hearing him holler wildly, only to find a shot has flashed just wide of the corner flag or out of the ground.

He does have an uncanny knack of getting things right though. In January 2020, he predicted live on air that Manchester City would win 5–0 at Aston Villa. I thought this was typical Charlie getting overexcited so repeated the outlandish prediction throughout the show. When Sergio Aguero scored their fifth after 57 minutes, my phone started to ping relentlessly with messages ranging from 'What score did Charlie go for mate?' from Tiss to 'Tee hee' from Thommo. It finished 6–1. So in the end Charlie (*ahem*) was hopelessly wrong.

Charlie is also one of the nicest men you will ever meet. It is hard to imagine anyone apart from a fan of Rangers or Tottenham disliking anything about him. Except of course that diamond stud in his ear.

Next to Chas, is Phil Thompson who in many ways I regard as the captain of the panel – well, certainly the elder statesman. He is on his second stint on the panel, broken only by a spell as assistant manager to Gerard Houllier at Liverpool. Thommo bleeds red – he has never in his life uttered the words 'Everton 2' – so that was a job he could never have turned down. He almost left for a second time when Houllier became Aston Villa manager and again wanted him as his right-hand man. But this was Villa, not Liverpool, and after a lot of soul searching, he decided to stay with Sky. I was delighted. I had spent a lot of time trying to persuade him not to leave. This was a huge decision as I am sure in his heart Phil suspected this might have been the last opportunity to be involved in the game in a hands-on way.

He was also a life-saver, quite literally, in 2019. A group of us were due to record a Sky Bet advert and Thommo and Tony Cottee were among those staying in our regular haunt, the Novotel in Brentford. Tony had gone to bed but was suffering terrible headaches and neck pain and vomiting. He rang Phil who went straight to his room. 'Flippin' heck. Look at the state of you!' was his reaction. A lot of people would have said get some rest and you will be okay. But Thommo, recognising the seriousness, went straight to reception and paid out of his own pocket for a private doctor to be called.

TC ended up in the West Middlesex and then Charing Cross hospitals. He had suffered a brain haemorrhage. Later Tony said, 'I will be forever grateful to him. He was there when I needed him.' I was grateful too. If anything had happened to TC, I would have been the shortest man on *Soccer Saturday*.

There has been talk in certain circles about Phil's age and whether football fans of a new generation can relate to him. My view is that if they are real football fans, even if they didn't see him play, they will still know about a man who captained his club and country, won 42 caps, 7 League titles, 3 Champions Leagues, 2 Uefa Cups, 2 League Cups and an FA Cup. Gary Lineker said recently that all the re-runs of classic, old football matches during the Covid-19 crisis had reminded the younger generation that he was famous for more than just advertising Walkers Crisps. But it was very much tongue in cheek. Real football fans will always remember the abilities of Lineker – and Thommo.

In my view, the likes of BBC Radio have made an error in their decision to sacrifice experience on the altar of youth. In recent times, talented broadcasters like Garry Richardson, Cornelius Lysaght, Mark Pougatch, Alan Green and Jonathan Overend have been allowed to leave as the Corporation tries to attract younger listeners. Do they not think that young people want to listen to intelligent, articulate people? I find that pretty insulting to the youth of today.

In broadcasting terms people get better with age (at least I hope so). The BBC just need to look at their own *Match of the Day* presenting team. Lineker has gone from hesitant beginner to a brilliant, polished performer. Alan Shearer has developed into one of the best pundits in the game. The same with Danny Murphy. Presenting, commentating and punditry is not as easy as it looks. Just watch most newcomers for proof of that.

Perhaps the most important point to consider of course is, if Thommo is deemed too old, how long have I got left?

Years ago, my then boss Vic Wakeling was unsure about Paul Merson as a panellist. 'How can we have a pundit who struggles to speak English?' But there is more than one way to skin a raccoon, as Merse would probably have put it.

I felt the public had an empathy with Merse. After all, how many of us speak the Queen's English? He has gone on to prove Vic wrong – and that has not happened too often. He tells it how he believes it is, frank and fearless. He may not always be right, but he is never afraid to give his opinion.

Merse has come a long way since his darkest days in the grip of booze and betting. But even then, he would never let the show down. There were times when I suspected he had barely been to bed, but when the red light went on, he would always be ready to make his points with a turn of phrase that only he could come up with:

'They are like a bag of Revels.'

'He's like a fish up a tree.'

'If you walk past the barbers every day, eventually you will get a haircut.'

'He's moving a bit sheeplessly.'

'They'll be doing carthorses if they score.'

I loved his description of why Newcastle United owner Mike Ashley would not be spending money in the transfer window:

'He wants to sell the club, so he ain't going to spend. If I knew I was going to divorce the wife, I wouldn't go out and buy her a new sofa!'

One day, Paul and I were shooting a TV advert for SkyBet. These are long, hard days with lines to be learned and lots of re-takes. Merse had been on a Fantasy Football end of season bash the previous night. When he got back home at dawn the following day, the car to take him to the studios was already waiting outside the front door of his home. He went in through the back door, came out the front and was driven to the shoot, where you would never have guessed what he had been up to the night before.

He was just as determined not to let down his local football side. He was playing at Wormwood Scrubs for a Sunday morning team. One Saturday he told me he was sub the next day. Sub? This was Paul Merson, ex-England and Arsenal. 'You're not going to turn up are you?' I asked. 'Of course I am. I can't let the boys down,' was his response.

If I need a straight, opinionated answer Paul is my go-to man. He is disarmingly honest. When I asked him about what he was missing most during the coronavirus lockdown, he said, 'My AA meetings.'

I used to think Merse was the perfect man's man. Liked a beer, liked a bet, and had some of the funniest stories you will ever hear. But the sort you wouldn't want your daughter bringing him home. These days, I think actually he is the sort you probably would want your daughter bringing home.

Matt Le Tissier sits next to me, in the position always reserved for flair players. Thommo has never sat in that chair. The likes of George Best, Rodney Marsh and David Ginola all have. Matt was a blindingly good footballer who deserved far more than the eight England caps he won. And he would be the first to tell you so! He would probably point out that Carlton Palmer won more than twice as many. It still winds Matt up. In my view though, every team needs a Carlton Palmer to do the work for those who don't like to do much running. Mind you, every Southampton fan would agree with Matt, the ultimate one-club man, who earned the nickname 'Le God' among Saints supporters and in one poll recently was named the Premier League's best-ever player. I looked to see if it was for the Premier League's best ever player from Guernsey, but no. That is quite an accolade when you think of Thierry Henry, Alan Shearer, Eden Hazard, Dennis Bergkamp and the rest.

Matt didn't need to do much running, partly down to his fabulous ability but also down to the fact that he is very quick-witted. He loves Twitter, but be careful if you take him on because he usually has a comeback:

> @Sam Youdale: Do you think you could get in the Southampton team now if you were in your prime?
>> @mattletiss7: You clearly didn't see me play in my prime.

> @reid6pete: What a intellectual challenging watch this is.
>> @mattletiss7: an intellectual, not a.

@aiden_lowton: Matt, you are a bellend.

  @mattletiss7: Thanks for following Aiden. Have a super evening.

@thomasgordon3: I loved him as a player and like him as a pundit. But I can't take any more of his stupidity. Time to unfollow!

  @mattletiss7: Twitter is not an airport. You don't have to announce your departure.

And he is never afraid to put his head above the parapet. After Southampton had won 4–0 at Portsmouth, he tweeted, 'That was a bit of a damp squib. I thought they might have given us a game,' thereby re-affirming his god-like status among Saints fans.

When Newcastle fans were attacking Mike Ashley (when weren't they?) Tiss tweeted, 'If the relegations were his fault, who takes the credit for the promotions?'

So you need to be at your sharpest to take on Matt in the *Soccer Saturday* studio, even on the day after Southampton had lost 9–0 at home to Leicester on Sky's *Live Friday Night Football*. Matt was at the game and so knew what was coming. In fact, on Saturday morning he texted asking for the day off as he wasn't feeling too well. Naturally, a record-breaking Premier League away win was the first topic of discussion. But it was also the day that England had beaten New Zealand 19–7 to reach the rugby World Cup final. Matt tried to deflect the discussion.

'Why are we wasting time talking about last night when we should be talking about England beating the All Blacks in the World Cup for goodness sake?'

Nice try (no pun intended) but I wasn't having it.

'And amazing to think Leicester scored more than the All Blacks.'

As @jordanriches put it on Twitter, 'RIP Matt Le Tissier!'

Of course Chris Kamara is the fifth Beatle. Rarely in the studio, he is the eyes and ears of the nation as he reports from one of the top games of the day, though at times he is a little deaf and a little short-sighted. Never more so than at Fratton Park when I crossed to him for news of a red card in the game between Portsmouth and Blackburn Rovers. 'But for who?' I asked.

'I don't know, Jeff, has there? I must have missed that. Red card?'

I tried again. 'Chris, have you not been watching? I don't know where it has come from. What has happened Chris?'

'I don't know, Jeff. I don't know. The rain must have got in my eyes, Jeff.'

'Chris, let me tell you, according to our sources, Anthony Vanden Borre has been sent off for a second bookable offence. Get your fingers out and count the number of Portsmouth players that are on the field.'

Finally realisation dawned on Kammy.

'No, you're right. I saw him go off but I thought they were bringing a sub on, Jeff.'

The incident went viral on the internet and on its 10th anniversary it produced a pretty similar reaction. Sky re-ran the clip, it made the national press and there were countless re-enactments of it on social media. It remains the greatest, funniest cock-up in the history of *Soccer Saturday* and probably of Sky Sports.

It is by no means the only thing he has missed. Reporting on a late Watford goal against Birmingham, Kammy told us breathlessly: 'I have just seen a marvellous, fantastic goal, a wonderful overhead kick goal that's put Watford in front. The only problem is that I am at the other end of the ground, so I don't know who scored it.'

And he has produced some wonderful one-liners:

'The atmosphere here is thick and fast.'

'Its 0–0, Jeff, but it could easily be the other way round.'

'He's got his legs on the wrong feet, Jeff.'

'If possession was five-tenths of the law . . .'

'Their energy has dispissipated [sic].'

'It is even Jeff, but Sunderland are on top.'

'Spurs are fighting like beavers!'

Not lions or tigers – too obvious for Kammy. It had to be those ferocious little beavers.

But make no mistake, Kammy has worked incredibly hard to get where he is. As well as his regular *Goals on Sunday* show, he hosts *Ninja Warrior UK* on ITV, he has made guest appearances on shows as varied as *Celebrity Juice* and *Emmerdale*, has been on stage with the Kaiser Chiefs and in 2019 had a Top 10 album with *Here's to Christmas*. He somehow finds time to fund-raise for Marie Curie Cancer Care. Everyone loves Kammy. Even though he made more than 600 league appearances as a footballer, it is his TV work that has established him as a national treasure.

A couple of years ago he and I were involved in travelling the length and breadth of Ireland for a series of online mini-documentaries in which we learned about Gaelic Football from scratch, leading up to us commentating on the All-Ireland Championship final at Croke Park in Dublin. I think it was on the first day that we realised how tough this would be when our first lesson was given to us by the legendary Irish commentator

Michael O'Muircheartaigh. You can imagine how well Kammy coped with that pronunciation. Thank goodness it wasn't Paul Merson.

For the best part of a week we raced around the country from Tralee to Carlow, from the amazing Aran Islands to over the border into Northern Ireland, watching different levels of the game. Neither of us could believe the incredible welcome. For the best part of a, week we knew what it felt like to live like Posh and Becks. By the final night I wanted a bit of peace and quiet, so suggested to the crew that we just stay in our smart hotel and have a quiet drink at the bar. Good plan. As Kammy and I pushed open the swing doors to the bar, flashlights popped and around 300 people gave us a standing ovation! Not such a good plan.

We had learned this is an astonishing sport, played at breakneck pace with amazing levels of fitness from players who are totally amateur. We also learned that referees needed eyes in the back of their heads. But I am not sure how much we knew about the nuances of the game.

We were back for the final in September, or at least I was. Kammy had to present *Goals on Sunday* in London. He assured me this was no problem. As soon as he was off the air, he was taken on the back of a motorbike to the nearest small airfield, flew to Dublin by private jet and jumped into a car to take him to Croke Park. He arrived one minute before kick-off.

We were treated to one of the greatest ever All-Ireland finals as red-hot favourites Dublin (the team everyone loves to hate) beat eternal runners-up Mayo thanks to a 40 metre free six minutes into stoppage time. As Kammy said as it flew between the posts, 'Unbelievable Jeff!'

It wasn't the first time I had been abroad with Kammy. We had been to the World Cup in Japan in 2002 and to the European Championships in Ukraine in 2012. I loved Kiev, though it is fair to say that the locals knew every scam in the book. On the first night, Kammy and I asked a taxi driver how much the fare would be to a bar that we had been told about. He quoted us about £30. We jumped in. He drove 50 yards up the road, did a U-turn and drove 50 yards back, stopping exactly opposite where he had picked us up. The bar had been literally just over the road from the rank.

We did a little pre-game entertainment for travelling England fans the following lunchtime. Among the audience was a man who asked if I would be so kind as to do an interview for Chinese TV. I was happy to oblige. He introduced me to their viewers.

'I am pleased to be joined today by Sky Sports presenter and former England footballer, Jeff Stelling.' It was a little awkward.

That evening we watched England beat Sweden in a brilliant game as guests of the FA. Somehow there were just three of us in an enormous hospitality box, me, Kammy and Noel Gallagher. By the end of the night it was clear Noel knew more about football than Chris and I put together!

A few years ago I made the basic error of agreeing to fly to Tenerife for Kammy's annual charity golf tournament and dinner. We were there for four days with just one round of golf and one dinner scheduled. So what could we possibly do the rest of the time? Suffice to say I was lucky not to be photographed in the same position as Jack Grealish had been on a visit to the island!

It is only recently that Kammy admitted to me that he could have been an international player too. I always thought of him as one of the Middlesbrough Kamaras. But it turns out that he was also one of the Sierra Leone Kamaras and was qualified to play for the African country. He was asked to play for them but turned the offer down. Imagine it – Kammy playing in the African Cup of Nations. Now that really would be unbelievable.

We had already been rotating the panel a little before the day at the end of August 2020 when things changed dramatically.

Thommo rang me to ask if I had any idea why he had been summoned to a Zoom call with Sky bosses later that morning. Charlie would be speaking to the hierarchy an hour later. We speculated that it could be that due to Covid they would not be allowed back into the studios for a time, or that something altogether more far-reaching was in the offing.

Just before noon my phone rang. I was stranded beside my car after suffering a puncture on the way to a recording session and was waiting for the AA. (Yes, I know what you are thinking, and I am *that* useless). It was Le Tiss.

'How are you?' I asked.

'Fine, until I was sacked five minutes ago,' was his reply. I knew then that the fate of Thommo and Charlie was also sealed. The only question remaining was whether I would be on the list. I wasn't.

I was gutted by the decisions, but in a long and sometimes difficult phone call, Rob Webster (Managing Director of Sky Sports) asked me to help build another team alongside Merse, a team that in years to come we might look on as fondly as George, Frank and Rodney or Charlie, Thommo and Le Tiss. I agreed and that is what everyone has been working hard to achieve, but it takes time.

Clinton Morrison is now a regular guest, always dressed to kill and always full of mischief. Tim Sherwood divides opinion. He holds strong views and is never afraid to air them. People tend to love him or hate him.

I am firmly in the first camp. In fact, in some ways he reminds me of Rodney Marsh. Ally McCoist is another who we use as often as his busy work schedule permits. His love of football, his love of life, his love of everything apart from former West Ham striker Sébastien Haller (suffice to say he did not rate him very highly) makes him a joy to work with. The effervescent Sue Smith is always a lot of fun: she packs her reports with passion and excitement.

We have been using Joleon Lescott more often. He certainly has the pedigree, having played for England, Manchester City, Wolves, Everton, West Brom and Aston Villa. He is quite thoughtful, which makes a nice change amongst our lot. Matt Murray is another who I expect will figure more in the future. More contemporary than most, he also has good contacts within the game. If only the former Wolves stopper had ever seen a goalkeeper make a mistake! He may be a former player, but he is definitely still a fully paid-up member of the keepers' union.

And we still have the likes of Alan McInally, or 'Munchen' as we know him, to call upon. (You may have heard him mention occasionally that he played for Bayern Munich! Though we take the mickey, that is some achievement.) If you want someone to spark a debate, he is often the man holding the firelighter.

Sometimes a guest can be an unexpected hit. That was certainly the case when Neil Warnock appeared on the panel. It was a risk as he tends to be Marmite within the game – some like him, some don't. His language on the touchline could be lively. And he and Thommo had a history of touchline confrontations. But he was a revelation.

On Manchester City: 'At Cardiff, after 33 minutes, I am on the touchline enjoying it and we are playing well. Eight minutes later we are 3–0 down. They score again and I am going "What a goal!" and I am the opposition manager.'

On Crystal Palace striker Alexander Sorloth (on loan at Trabzonspor): 'To be fair if you had seen him at Palace, you would have played yourself before him. A toss-up between that or the kit man.'

On Wolves: 'They have the worst backroom staff I have ever come across on the touchline. Every decision 10 of them get around the fourth official. They take it in turns to have a go at him. To be fair, I had a good chat with Nuno and he is a good manager. It's his staff that I can't stand!'

On Newcastle 0 Burnley 0 (the game he was watching in the studio): 'Please don't keep coming to me Jeff if you can help it.'

Newcastle 0 Burnley 0, FT: 'The most exciting thing

today was the chicken and mayo sandwich. Thanks for asking me to come here from Cornwall.'

It is a good job he had the chicken and mayo sandwich. At Sky, the BLT usually turns out to be more of an LT. Sometimes it is pretty much just an L. And don't get me started on the wallpaper paste soup. After a quarter of a century I still have not worked out what flavour it is really meant to be. At least it does not come with twigs in it, as one of the chef's specials appears to.

Social media went crazy over Neil:

> @HeathTaylor: Neil Warnock on Soccer Saturday, a breath of fresh air, so funny.

> @Jackjackcoop93: Just when you think Saturdays can't get any better they've got Neil Warnock on Soccer Saturday. What a character!

> @HarryWilko1: Somehow I hate this guy but love him at the same time.

> @as_it_is10: When he has a job he is an utter knob, but when he is out of work he is absolute class.

> @Murton_Red: As a manager I couldn't stand the twisty moaning old git but as a pundit he is great coz he doesn't give a flying fig about upsetting anyone.

@hola_jase: Thanks for asking me to come from Cornwall today... Absolute banger.

@joeforman6: What a legend. You can't not like this man.

@steviehammer: Needs to be a regular. Warnock has many haters but I can't help but like him. Straight talking, no nonsense old school moaner, but knows so much about the game and has a fantastic record to back it up.

More Marmite please.

4

MRS BROWN'S BOYS

It was during a commercial break, at about half-past-four one Saturday, that a copy of the e-mail was thrust in front of me. It just read, 'I am Mrs Brown and those are my boys. I am recovering at home from an operation and watch the show every week to see if they have scored.'

'One of Mrs Brown's boys has scored!' has become one of the new – well, newer – *Soccer Saturday* catch-phrases.

A couple of seasons ago Scott Brown, Jordan Brown and Jason Brown were all playing for Peterhead in Scottish Division Two and were frequently among the goals. Actually, only two of the three were really Mrs Brown's Boys. Jason is Jordan's younger brother, but Scott is no relation. Still, why let that get in the way of a good line (he is obviously still one of Mrs Brown's boys – just a different Mrs Brown).

Like any other programme, *Soccer Saturday* has had to move with the times. Some of those catchphrases listed in my earlier book *Jelleyman's Thrown a Wobbly* have become redundant, ironically including the book's title, as Gareth Jelleyman is now in his forties and I doubt his name will appear on the vidiprinter again. Famously, he was sent off playing for Mansfield against Cheltenham just as full-time scores were coming through at machine-gun pace. At that moment, I didn't care about the Manchester United or Arsenal results. This might be my only chance to deliver a line I had saved for seasons. 'Jelleyman's been sent off for Mansfield. Let's hope he hasn't thrown a wobbly.' It was the first and last time the phrase appeared on *Soccer Saturday*.

Other old favourites have become obsolete too. The Good Doctor Kenny Deuchar is presumably now doctoring full-time as opposed to part-time as he was when playing for Gretna; the last dance has long since taken place in the streets of Total Network Solutions; James Brown stopped feeling good – injuries forced him into premature retirement; Kevin's sisters, the Nolans, no longer felt like dancing as Kev had hung up his boots. There are still a few Stevensons/Stephensons playing, so thankfully 'Stevenson/Stephenson – must have been a Rocket', which has been around as long as the show itself, still gets the occasional outing.

My favourite was 'Lisa will be happy' every time Adam Stansfield scored for Yeovil or Exeter or Hereford. But tragically he passed away in 2010, aged just 31.

Judge for yourself if the 2020 generation of catch-phrases live up to – or down to – the originals:

> *'EISA OPENS HIS ACCOUNT,*
> *YOU CAN BANK ON HIM,*
> *WHAT A GREAT INVESTMENT'*
> *(Optional addition near transfer window –*
> *'THERE'S BOUND TO BE INTEREST IN HIM')*

Mo Eisa is a striker who plays for Peterborough and I was pretty pleased with myself when I first came up with it. With 16 goals by the end of February, even I was tiring of hearing it. It's a catchphrase not without controversy as some commentators started to pronounce it Eesa not Isa, which ruins the gag. Thankfully, when one of my *Soccer Saturday* colleagues asked him about it during the course of an interview, he obligingly replied, 'Jeff can pronounce it whichever way he wants!'

> *'A JUNIOR EISA, YOU CAN BANK ON HIM,*
> *WHAT . . .'*

. . . well you know the rest. There is a god! And there is a Junior Eisa, Mo's young brother Abo, who has been playing for Scunthorpe United.

'BOWIE IS AN ABSOLUTE BEGINNER, BUT HE'S THE STARMAN AND FAME AND GOLDEN YEARS LIE AHEAD'

Keiron Bowie is a teenage striker playing for Roath Ravers. People still think it's a slip of the tongue when I call them Roath by the way, even though I have done it hundreds of times over the last decade. The club even sent me a mug with Roath Ravers emblazoned on it.

'WHAT SORT OF GOAL WAS IT? IT WAS A BEAUTYMAN!'

Dedicated to Harry Beautyman, of National League Sutton United. Although when he scored twice at Victoria Park against Hartlepool in the 2019–20 season, I am sure they were scruffy, jammy goals.

'ANDY WILLIAMS SCORES AGAIN – IT'S TOO GOOD TO BE TRUE'

The Northampton Town striker shares his name with one of the great crooners of the 60s and 70s. He has scored nearly 150 goals during his career, yet no-one has ever paid a penny for him, clearly believing that goalscoring record *is* too good to be true.

'JACOBS HAS SCORED – IT'S A CRACKER'

(Interchangeable with
'CRAWFORD HAS SCORED –IT'S A CRACKER')

More often than not this is used when Keaghan Jacobs, Livingston's record appearance holder, scores. But I deliciously suckered in the gullible Charlie Nicholas recently when Kyle Jacobs scored for Morton against Partick Thistle. 'Jacobs has scored. What sort of goal do you think it was?' I asked. Charlie came back in a flash. 'A cracker!' 'No,' I said. 'It was a penalty'.

'ARCHIE MCPHEE SCORES
– HIS NANNY WILL BE PLEASED'

It is one that is used relatively rarely as Archie is not the most prolific goal scorer in Scottish football. This can be amended to Scarlett will be pleased, when Kevin O'Hara scores for Alloa Athletic.

'IT'S PRINGLE – MUST HAVE BEEN A CRISP FINISH'

Used even more sparingly – in fact, it is almost obsolete – as Ben Pringle hasn't scored since March 2018. He is at Gillingham and I am desperate for the chance to dust it down and deliver it just once more.

'SURELY KEITH COULD ASK SOME OF HIS
MATES TO HELP'

Used exclusively when the Highland League side get a drubbing after reaching the Scottish Cup proper.

'FLANAGAN AND ANNAN
– ALWAYS GO TOGETHER WELL'

This is as near to subtle as *Soccer Saturday* gets. (Too subtle in fact for show director Caroline Eccles, who just doesn't get it. But then she is from Preston.) Raith Rovers loaned Nathan Flanagan to Annan Athletic in the 2019–2020 season to allow this reference to Flanagan and Allen, the legendary double act who were responsible for classics like 'Run Rabbit Run' and 'Underneath the Arches'. It could be a generational thing that some don't understand the reference. Of course Thommo and I both do!

'BEWARE O'WARE AS THEY SAY AT MORTON'

Thomas O'Ware played for Morton and now Partick Thistle. When he scores I always say, 'Beware O'Ware as they say at Morton.' Charlie Nicholas always insists they say no such thing. But with 28 goals in 238 games – not too shabby for a defender – if they don't perhaps they should.

'ONE POTATO, TWO POTATO, EKPITETA'

Used when the Leyton Orient defender pops up for any reason. Juvenile I know, but I love it.

And one that has yet to be used but is waiting in the wings:

'NAUGHTY NAUGHTY NORTEI NORTEY'

In five years and more than 150 appearances for the likes of Dover, Solihull Moors and Chorley in the National League, he has never been red-carded. If it ever happens, it could be the new Jelleyman moment. As it stands, it is just a waste of a great name!

I'm also waiting for Grant Savoury to score his first goal. He's on loan at Edinburgh City. But if they want to buy him, do they go to parent club Celtic or Greggs?

I like to keep records too of players who haven't scored for a long time, but like the catchphrases, they also change. Sometimes agonisingly. For example, I had been keeping track of Josh McEachran over the years. He started at Chelsea and had loan spells at the likes of Middlesbrough, Watford and Wigan. But it was at Brentford that he found a home. I noticed that he had never scored a club goal and started to make a note each week. 'McEachran 0 in 101,' I would scribble next to Brentford. '0 in 130', '0 in 170' and so it went on, week after week, game after game.

I will never ever forget the traumatic night it happened. Tuesday 2 October 2018. At just before half-past-eight. I was sitting at home watching Julian Warren host a midweek *Soccer Special* when to my horror the vidi-printer spelled out what had happened. Brentford 1 (Josh McEachran) Birmingham City 1. He had scored at the 189th time of asking and he had done it when I wasn't presenting the show! Two years of keeping count and making notes wasted. Honestly, I was gutted. I was even more gutted when they showed the goal, and with apologies to Josh, it was a fluke. He took a free-kick from around 25 yards out on the right-hand side, and his floated cross went straight through the keeper's hands. At least that's how it looked to me through my moist eyes.

Another change involves games played during the show. After all, six hours is a long time. I am sure plenty still play the legendary drinking game, where contestants have to take a drink every time a certain phrase is used (not that I could possibly endorse it!). After all, Kammy still says 'Unbelievable Jeff', Merse still uses 'Desmond' and 'He has hit the Beans', and I still make bad gags about A triallist and his brothers B and C tri-allist, so there's still plenty of opportunity to imbibe. I hope no-one is waiting for me to say 'The Good Doctor' again or they could go thirsty. Hopefully, the rules have been rewritten and updated.

But virtually every week now we get letters, e-mails and tweets from people with another reason to watch carefully. Stag and hen parties and birthday bashes increasingly seem to rely on where the first goal to appear on the vidiprinter has been scored. If it's Scunthorpe United 1 Southend 0, it is off to Scunthorpe for the bash. The more conservative will head there in a week or so, but the real risk-takers gather in a pub next to their local railway station waiting for the first goal to go in and then head off on the first train after three o'clock heading in vaguely the right direction. I am sure they are hoping it is going to a London club, or Man U or Man City. Liverpool perhaps? Newcastle United (not likely) or maybe Rangers or Celtic? More often than not though, it is Scunthorpe! (Please don't be offended Scunthorpians, I could have picked many places.)

The Sky Jolly Boys, a group of football-loving Sky workers in Scotland, decided on their annual trip away this year on the same basis. It turned out that they were off to Blackpool, which didn't seem too bad to me. And in August, it would have been fine. But this was February and as they told me afterwards, Blackpool was closed!

My rant many years ago about a TV show's criticism of Middlesbrough still gets shown at some events that I go to. But that's something else that has had to move on. Of course with the introduction of VAR, these days there are plenty of opportunities (don't get me started, we only have a couple of hundred pages). But it was

September 2018 when I last had a proper rant – and again it was about my native Northeast, but this time Newcastle.

Look I do love the earlier days, but I am not a professional Northeasterner who won't hear a word said against the region. Like everywhere else, it has good and bad. But Ian Abrahams, the Moose on talkSPORT, had picked a bad target when he had a go at Newcastle, the city, as opposed to Newcastle United, the football club. I suspect Moose was being no more than a little mischievous when he said on air that the only reason there are 52,000 at St James' Park for home games is because there is nothing else to do. This made him instantly on a par with Mike Ashley in terms of popularity among Geordies.

I took the chance to have a bit of a go on *Soccer Saturday*. Well, quite a lot of a go actually.

'You may have seen that a radio reporter said that the only reason Newcastle get 52,000 is because there is nothing else to do in the city. Well, this is not a rant, but . . .

'He has probably never been to St James' Park.

'He has probably never had a big night out in the Bigg Market.

'He has probably never eaten at any of the wonderful restaurants.

'He has never appreciated the marvellous architecture of Grey Street.

'He will never have been to the Theatre Royal.

'Never been to the racecourse.

'He will never have strode along the Quayside in the shadow of the Tyne Bridge.

'I doubt he has ever visited the Baltic Gallery.

'He probably doesn't know that Greggs opened their first ever branch in Newcastle in 1951.

'He has never had a Newky Brown.

'He has never had a Stottie cake – actually he has probably eaten a Stottie cake, quite a lot of them in fact.

'It's a wonderful city with loads to do, loads to eat and loads to drink. Don't believe what you hear on the radio. Trust me.'

In truth it was easy to defend Newcastle. For me, it's not just one of the best cities in England but one of the best in Europe. In truth, I felt more than a little sorry for Moose, who works hard and has done brilliantly at talkSPORT. He was just trying to make a headline. And he did. It was a brutal one at the *Mag*, Newcastle United's influential independent fan site.

JEFF STELLING TEARS TALKSPORT IDIOT APART – QUALITY

I have to admit I felt a little guilty.

5

GIRLS ALLOWED

Looking at all the correspondence I get, one of the things that stands out is how many female football fans there are now compared to the days when I made my first tentative steps in sports broadcasting. It's very much a change for the better, if you ask me.

I was about seven when I first harangued and cajoled my big sister, Sue, into taking me to a football match (Hartlepool obviously). I can just about guarantee you that she was the only woman in the ground. It was just not the norm. I am not even sure there was a women's toilet in the ground.

Sue was no football fan and I know she did not enjoy the intimidatory atmosphere. She was simply doing her sisterly duty. Even in the 1970s and '80s when I was a reporter for the BBC and LBC, there was a dearth of women at matches. It wasn't that surprising. Some grounds were bear pits, violence was common, language appalling and facilities diabolical.

And you would certainly not find a woman in the press box.

Sue died tragically early in her mid-thirties, but I think if she was still alive she would approve if she was to visit a ground now. She would not be the only woman for a start. These days grounds are thankfully awash with families which can only be a good thing.

Thinking back to my early days on LBC/IRN and at the BBC, there was not a single female broadcaster on either sports desk. There were female producers, who were occasionally allowed to appear on air by reading the racing results but nothing more.

Now *Soccer Saturday* has almost as many female viewers as men, and the correspondence and fan mail that the programme gets is certainly reflected in that. More and more women are making their mark in football broadcasting. I'll be honest here. Until recently, I didn't believe a woman would ever be on our panel on the show. I wasn't a sexist. For around 18 months, Helen Rollason and I were a couple. Thirty years ago, she was a trailblazer along with Sue Barker and Hazel Irvine in terms of women making a career from sports broadcasting. She knew she had to work harder, be better and make fewer errors than her male counterparts just to be treated as an equal in some people's eyes. Helen wasn't a particularly radical or strident feminist, but she certainly wouldn't have allowed me to get away with any displays of sexism, and nor would I have expected her to. It's just at the time I could not see where that female pundit was going to come from. There was no career path. No-one was getting a chance. Now they are. Just look at what the peerless Clare Balding has achieved. Starting as a trainee with BBC Radio, she has established herself as one of the country's foremost presenters, not just on sport but shows like *Countryfile* and *Crufts*.

Sue Smith is, for me, the best example of a woman who fits in perfectly on *Soccer Saturday*. Not surprisingly she was nervous when she first started. In fact, a lot of the women we approached to try out on our midweek shows were wary, because those who had appeared were being savaged on social media – regardless of whether they were good, bad or indifferent. Sue is a Scouser, so it goes without saying she can talk and has bags of personality, but she also works hard at her prep on whichever game she is doing. Too many people, men and women, think they can turn up, sit down and talk about a game without having done any homework. Sue is now a regular on *Soccer Special* and doing the early or late game on *Soccer Saturday*. It's lovely to have an Evertonian in the studio to combat Thommo's Liverpool bias.

Our reporters Bianca Westwood, Michelle Owen and Faye Carruthers are as good as any of either sex in the game. Bianca was the first woman to appear 'in vision' for *Soccer Saturday* and over the years we have developed a bit of repartee, but as a presenter you have to be careful. Bianca can get away with calling me short, fat or old – which she does most weeks. But when I and the panel laughed as she was getting blown away by the nearest thing to a hurricane that Dagenham has ever seen while she was reporting on their game against Scunthorpe, we had to weather a social media storm from people condemning us as sexist. It was ridiculous. We would have been exactly the same had it been Tony Cottee at the game.

On another occasion, when Bianca was interviewing a player in the twilight of his career, she ended the report by telling him, 'Never mind, none of us will ever be as old as Jeff Stelling!' I couldn't think of a quick put down in response and was being heckled by the panel, when I realised what date it was. 'We have to let Bianca have her say on this special day for her,' I said. 'Halloween!' Cue outrage – not from Bianca, not from those who think age is just a number, but from those who thought it was a dig too far.

A handful of people even complained of sexism when during a Millwall game we cut to Bianca but only half her head was in vision. We could see her lips move, but there was nothing above her mouth! Not surprisingly we laughed. But could you imagine it being any different if it had happened to Kammy instead? Of course not.

Bianca is never offended and does not want people to be offended on her behalf. She also gives more than her fair share back. I remember her killing me when Saturday fell on 14 February with, 'It's a fantastic game Jeff and makes up for me having to spend my Valentine's Day with you!'

Her favourite match though must have been when she was sent to cover Stevenage against Hartlepool. I was like a Cheshire cat when we took the lead after four minutes. Six Stevenage goals later, Bianca ended her final report with, 'I almost feel sorry for you. Almost!'

Michelle and Faye are more recent recruits. Michelle recently had her first child, Zac, but I was horrified with the abuse she had to take leading up to his birth. She worked on screen until almost the last minute – in fact she almost gave birth at a Swansea game, I think – but trolls came up with some abhorrent abuse over her appearance in her final couple of months of pregnancy. It is so unfair. As if that wasn't bad enough she has also come in for social media abuse meant for Michael Owen!

'I am going to have to change my handle to NOT Michael Owen,' she tweeted.

Michelle is going to have to change her drink as well. She revealed recently her favourite tipple is Malibu and Coke. Matt Le Tissier and Michelle will have to stand at the other end of the bar from me when we next have a night out . . .

I am sure Bianca and Faye would agree with Michelle when she says, 'I am football reporter and presenter. I don't prefix that with woman. I am here on ability not gender.' It's about time people accepted that. None of the women on our team want preferential treatment. They just want equal treatment.

People like Sky's golf reporter and presenter Sarah Stirk, Tamsin Greenway on netball and cricket's Isa Guha are just superb broadcasters. Isa has made the breakthrough in a sphere that was previously pretty much exclusively male. If cricket and golf, for so long bastions of male chauvinism can accept change, why can't football?

Radio, which was once devoid of women broadcasters, has now realised there is a significant pool of female talent out there. TalkSPORT now has Laura Woods, Georgie Bingham and Natalie Sawyer. I loved Nat putting a fan in his place recently as he derided her for not watching her team Brentford, home and away. (Don't you just hate fans who think they are superior because they can do that?) She pointed out that she is a working mum with a young son who doesn't especially like football, which makes it impossible for her to get to away games. It's something most men don't have to think about. It doesn't make her any less of a football fan or any less capable of talking intelligently about it.

Of course, one of the most common accusations levelled at the new wave of women commentators is that their views are devalued because they have never played men's professional football. That should rule me out too. But you try stopping me telling Thommo that he is wrong. Nothing irritates me more than when people tell me I can't really understand the game because I have never played it. It is so condescending.

I had first-hand experience of the problems facing women working as football presenters with Rachel Riley on *Friday Night Football*. Having worked with Rach on *Countdown*, I was very much in favour of the plan to pair us as co-hosts when Sky showed live Premier League football on Fridays for the first time. It wasn't easy. There were very few live games so it was hard for either of us to find a rhythm. I also felt the two-handed presentation didn't work. Producers would try to choreograph questions but you simply can't conduct interviews like that. If I got an answer to a question that I felt demanded a follow-up, I couldn't as it was Rachel's turn. The shows were far from disasters, but equally far from the vision we all had.

Rachel took more than her fair share of criticism from keyboard warriors, but things became intolerable after Spurs had lost at West Ham in a key game in their bid to win the title. In the after-match debate, Rachel commented: 'It is déjà vu for Spurs isn't it? A proper bottle job.'

If I or either of our studio guests, Jamie Redknapp and Thierry Henry, had made the remark, I think we would have incurred the wrath of some Tottenham fans but nothing more. By contrast Rachel received hideous personal abuse on social media. At the end of the season, she decided she didn't want to carry on.

Friday Night Football reverted to one-person presentation hosted by Kelly Cates, another fine broadcaster whose success has nothing to do with her sex. She is just bloody good at the job.

6

YOU BET!

When I first started working for SkyBet, I would have offered anyone 33–1 against me singing on a Christmas TV advert.

But the bookies always win in the end, so there I was, a couple of years back, with a Lee Marvin-esque, practically talking version of 'It's the Most Wonderful Time of the Year' as part of their Christmas campaign.

I would have also given you a big price against me appearing dressed as a thickly bearded Santa Claus with supporting dancing elves Matt Le Tissier, Charlie Nicholas and Phil Thomson – but it had happened the previous festive season. It would have been long odds too against me welcoming people to my fictional abode, Stelling Towers, stashing my hoard of Super Six gold bars while dressed in a red velvet smoking jacket and with the help of my butler. Or fleeing from a stampede of Cheltenham festival runners (and overtaking Jamie Carragher – but then who hasn't?). Or standing in an ill-fitting, sparkling gold suit, arms akimbo, holding scales that looked like they had been used at Arkwright's in a previous life. That would have been quite an accumulator!

Holding those scales up by the way was impossible. I had to have a specially designed stand to balance them on after every single take, and by the end of the advert I had arms like Sylvester Stallone in *Rambo*.

It is fair to say though that my association with SkyBet, who I have worked with for several years now, has caused me more than a little grief. Some people have strong opinions over gambling and have expressed their views in no uncertain terms.

To Jeff Stelling (cc Head of Sport),

What an utterly loathsome individual you really are – Smelling would be a far more appropriate surname. You come onto our screens in various ridiculous clothes, on some occasions looking like a lord of the manor, complete with large portrait of you on the wall, then in a gaudy gold suit, both to promote the social cancer that is gambling. And your pathetic tag line for SkyBet is making betting better. You level no playing fields, nor zap any asterisks by promoting the payment of winning bets in cash, not free bets. What you really do is make the lives of many unfortunate individuals, some quite young, intolerable. Like the loathsome Ray Winstone, you are clearly a very greedy, self-centred individual and, in your case, one who seems to assuage his conscience by appealing for donations in support of prostate cancer research, but no please or thank you. I hope Sky Sports give you what you deserve – the boot and pronto. Finally you have a glib, smirking superficial manner which I know many viewers find nauseating. Go back to Hartlepool and take up deep sea fishing and ideally do it when storms are forecast!

Yours against gambling promotion,

I Dogood

At least I Dogood did gooder than Nonie Insall who addressed her letter to 'Geoff Stelling' and who clearly got me mixed up with another TV hardman with the following line:

I have become increasingly concerned by your regular presence on the gambling website Bet 365.

Now I accept that I might have had a passing resemblance to Ray Winstone when he used to pop up in *Minder* from time to time. But he is from East London, I am from Northeast England. He is a West Ham fan, I am a Hartlepool fan. He is hard, I am not (probably).

It's not the worst case of mistaken identity I have ever been involved in though. Waiting for my luggage at Gatwick airport, I was approached by a man who had clearly enjoyed his flight home from wherever a little too much.

'I recognise you, don't I?' he asked.

'Not sure, do you?'

'You're that bloke off the telly!'

'I am,' I said modestly, but nevertheless secretly quite pleased to have been recognised in front of my family, even by someone who has clearly had one, or two, too many.

'I just can't remember the name. Give me a clue.'

'Do you like football?' Big clue delivered.

'Oh, got it. You're Trevor Brooking!'

Cue my sons dropping their cases, doubled up with laughter. Sir Trevor Brooking is about six inches taller than me, two stones lighter and unlike me, was a brilliant footballer (though I could probably head it as well as Trev could).

The blame for promoting gambling was not always laid firmly at the door of Ray or me. Sometimes the burden was shared.

Dear Messrs Stelling and Kamara,
    It would appear that you are a pair of seriously

greedy broadcasters, like Lineker, Norton and Evans of the BBC. At least your vast earnings don't come from the licence fee payers. What is particularly disgusting is your promotion of gambling (SkyBet and Ladbrokes). Maybe Mr Stelling you think in some sort of twisted way that your support for prostate cancer research compensates. No doubt you give money to charity as I do, but now with your twisted faces appearing on Gillette ads, the pair of you really do appear to be a pair of seriously greedy/avaricious individuals. More, more, more . . . be ashamed, very ashamed and if it is possible more discerning in your advertising choices.

Yours disgusted,

Jim Black

PS That guy Ben Shepherd I am told reliably brags about being sent off in a Charity fund raiser. Quite disgraceful and if true he should be fired by Sky and ITV with his pathetic tipping point programme.

Poor Ben! How did he get dragged into all of this?

Look I understand how emotive the subject of gambling and the advertising of it can be. A lot of high-profile footballers – the likes of Matthew Etherington, Keith Gillespie and Michael Chopra – have lost fortunes over the years. I work with Paul Merson of course, who has suffered from a gambling addiction.

From the day he won his first professional contract, Merse was gambling away his wages. He would race off the pitch at half-time to find out how that day's bets were doing. He lost millions.

When he became a panellist on *Soccer Saturday*, Merse would arrive at Sky Sports on Saturday mornings and ask what I thought of Forfar Athletic's chances at Brechin City. When I professed to having no idea, he would tell me that half of Brechin's team were working that day, including their top scorer. He was trying to convince himself as much as me. Whenever he was not on the air he was glued to his smartphone, and when he says, 'I was getting up in the morning and betting on Lithuanian Under-20s basketball matches,' he wasn't joking.

I remember one day sharing a car with him en route to recording the *Soccer Saturday Christmas Special*, which that year was a golf tournament. It was 6.30 in the morning but Merse was already on his phone placing a bet. 'On what?' I asked. It turned out to be the semi-finals of the Chinese Ladies doubles tennis championship and Merse had backed Wing and Wong to beat Ying and Yang! I never thought of him as a problem gambler.

He didn't have a notice on his forehead saying so and we heard about the occasional big wins. But, of course, not the regular heavy losses. 'You go insane. You search and search for the bet and then you think, "Why did I do that?"' he says. But somehow, though it affected his life it didn't affect his performances on the pitch and it didn't affect his performances on *Soccer Saturday*.

I am pleased to say Paul has beaten, or at least, is beating his gambling demons. He even declines to get involved in our *Soccer Saturday* football accumulator where every week we each put in £20 and pick one sure-fire, can't lose, usually odds-on certainty. We have won once in three years! The boys on the panel admire how he has battled his demons and love him for the person he is.

It is not just footballers of course. For years I worked with 'Mr 147' Willie Thorne covering snooker for Sky. Willie had earned his nickname for the number of max-imums he had rolled in over the years. He was always charming company in the TV presentation studio, immaculately dressed, almost debonair, and had a love for the better things in life. Montrachet was his tipple. But gambling was his weakness. The sessions at snooker were often long and there was always an on-site bookie. We would pass some of the time there. But to be honest if I had bet on a horse, I always hoped it wouldn't be the one to beat Willie's in a photo finish. My tenner didn't matter. His stake – he never told us how much – certainly would.

I remember once watching a race with Willie and a number of the production staff. I knew he had lumped heavily on the favourite. When it jumped the last 10 lengths clear, everyone was ready to celebrate. But somehow on the run in, the horse's weight cloth flew off. As it passed the winning post, the inevitable stewards inquiry was announced. Willie knew the horse would automatically be disqualified. One of the Sky crew, well-intentioned but unfamiliar with the racing game, tried to console him before the official announcement. 'Never mind, Willie,' she said. 'It might still keep the race.' I could have cried for him. Willie was the unluckiest gambler I ever met. In total he lost more than a million pounds over the years,

I was greatly saddened to learn of his premature death in Spain at the age of just 66. Let's be honest, snooker was not always the most thrilling sport. Not every match was a re-run of the Dennis Taylor against Steve Davis World Championship final in 1985. More often than not it would be slow going until late into the night at the Motherwell Concert Hall or Plymouth Pavilions. Willie helped keep me sane with his great stories and conversation until we could eventually escape for a beer or, in his case, a glass of white. He was one of snooker's great characters, on and off the green baize.

A couple of years ago, SkyBet arranged for me to interview the former Reading, Oxford and Crawley player Scott Davies at a Football League meeting. They wanted him to speak directly to those within football of the dangers facing wealthy, young men with time and money on their hands. Scott told me that he had gambled away his entire £30,000 signing-on fee within three weeks of getting it. He knows his addiction cost him the chance to have a potentially lucrative, glittering career. Now he spends much of his time travelling around the country, delivering talks at football clubs.

So I recognise the dangers of gambling.

I support the removal of slot machines from betting shops, the reduction of the maximum stake/winnings for them.

I have concerns about online casinos. During the coronavirus crisis, TV viewers were swamped with adverts enticing them to play online slots or roulette. SkyBet asked me to record an online advert pointing out the dangers of people getting drawn into this type of gambling simply due to boredom.

I know a lot of people feel bombarded by betting adverts around live sporting events and the reduction of those should also be applauded.

I was nevertheless astonished when an advert I fronted for SkyBet's 'Request A Bet' was banned by the

Advertising Standards Authority on the basis that it implied having sporting knowledge could enhance your chance of placing a winning bet. I would argue that it is an advantage to know Liverpool have a better football team than Macclesfield Town. Or that Richard Johnson is a fine jockey. Or that Lewis Hamilton is a brilliant driver of a Formula One car. Having knowledge of those things must improve your chances of having a winning bet, obviously without guaranteeing it. Not surprisingly the ruling was overturned on appeal and the ban was lifted.

A lot of bookmakers now have deposit limits, cooling off periods and even telephone potential problem gamblers. Charlie, Tiss and Thommo took part in the 'Three simple tools' advertising campaign for SkyBet promoting just those things. It is no longer possible now to bet by credit card – again a good move.

The problem is many people love to gamble, whether it is the lottery, bingo, horse racing or Super Six. These days I am as likely to hear people in the street shout, 'Where's the briefcase?' or 'Where's the million?' as 'Unbelievable Jeff!' – well almost as likely. It is a difficult one and I can't pretend to know what the answer is. Some people have suffered terribly through gambling. But if we ban TV advertising, would that include the lottery? It may help good causes, but it is a form of gambling.

Those who want a complete ban on gambling have to consider the number of jobs that would be lost in the racing industry as well as the betting companies themselves. That would run to tens of thousands.

But there is another side to all of this. Over the years more than £10 million has been won on Super Six on *Soccer Saturday*. I remember ringing £250,000 winner David White live on the programme to tell him he had won. He was so gobsmacked, I could hardly get a word out of him. And I will never forget travelling to a swanky hotel in the south of England to meet our first £1 million jackpot winners, a young couple who were not even aware that they had won until the following day.

Grace, who was in her twenties, had put her selections on, gone to work and forgotten about it. Her partner worked overnight shelf-stacking in a local superstore. He had worked that Saturday evening, not realising they had predicted six correct scores and hit the jackpot.

Their joy was unbridled. But they were also humble and grateful. They didn't have their own home and had never been abroad. In fact neither had ever flown. They were the perfect winners, their lives changed for ever and hopefully very much for the better.

I was brought up in a family that loved a flutter. But my Dad was a steelworker and his idea of reckless was to have a 20p round robin. Our family holidays weren't jaunts to the Costa Del Sol – my mum lived until she was 96 and had never been on an airplane – but day trips to Redcar, Ripon, Thirsk and Beverley, which all have racecourses. Again I learned restraint from my dad who had a maximum stake of £1 per race. I never bet an amount that it would upset me to lose.

My love of racing meant that when Sky launched their live evening racing show *The Winning Post* I was asked to host it. During the summer months I presented live on three evenings a week from tracks as far apart as Hamilton and Brighton. It was a lot of fun, but again not everyone appreciated me!

I received a letter – which I didn't keep for reasons that will soon become obvious – from a punter who told me he wanted to 'wipe the sickly, smug smile off my face with the toe of his boot'.

My wife Lizzie, then PA to the MD of Sky Sports, Vic Wakeling, had developed a delicious way of dealing with abusive complaints about presenters. She simply wrote back, enclosing an autographed photo of the subject of the complaint with a note saying, 'Thank you for your interest in Sky Sports. Please enjoy the signed photo of Jeff,' or whoever it may be. I thought I would develop this a little further, so next time *The Winning Post* was on, I read out the letter. And the writer's name. And his full address.

The address was in Musselburgh, just outside Edinburgh, which itself has a racetrack. A couple of weeks later I was hosting *The Winning Post* from there. Just before we were due to go on air, I saw a couple of large, tattooed, shaven-headed guys striding towards me. I feared the worst. Was one of this pair the man who wanted to wipe the sickly, smug smile off my face? As we were about to go on the air, I couldn't run or hide, I just had to face the music.

As the men reached me, the first towered above me. Not difficult, I know.

'Jeff,' he said. 'Ah just wanted to tell ye, that guy who wanted to wipe the sickly, smug smile off yer face. He'll nae be bothering ye again.'

I was relieved and terrified in the same moment. I got rid of the letter that night. And I never did hear from him again.

'When the Fun Stops, STOP!' the commercials implore us. And I did stop. I never read out anyone's home address again!

7

LOVE BITES AND EVERYTHING

Dear Jeff,

Re: Sports Broadcaster of the Year

Congratulations on your recent award from the Sports Journalists Association.

Being recognised as 'Sports Broadcaster of the Year' is a great accolade but to win it four years in a row is an incredible feat.

Consecutive awards are a tribute to talent and a remarkable consistency and I wanted to add my praise to that of your many admirers. I know you pay tribute to the team around you on Soccer Saturday, the way you all entertain and inform our viewers live, throughout the afternoon deserves the highest praise. And the fun is infectious even for a Newcastle fan.

I am glad you continue to receive the thoroughly deserved recognition of your peers.

Best regards,

Jeremy

The letter was from Sky's Chief Executive Jeremy Darroch and I have kept it to this day. I went on to win the award for a fifth successive year. But the Sports Journalists' Association changed the rules after that so that the award was voted on by a select panel rather than the rank and file of their membership. Not only have I not won the award again, I have not even been nominated. It makes me think my form must have fallen off the edge of a cliff. Or that the *Soccer Saturday* team had done a Bolton Wanderers, tumbling from top division to the fourth level of the English game.

But looking back, I still think we have been the form team. Of course, there are great memories from the early years of *Soccer Saturday* – Rodney Marsh's impetuous pledge that he would have his head shaved if Bradford survived in the Premier League among them. They did and he did! Matt Le Tissier's unmerciful taunting of Phil Thompson when Liverpool fell behind at home to Havant & Waterlooville in the FA Cup. My Middlesbrough rant when the Channel 4 programme *Location, Location, Location* dubbed it the worst place to live in

England (with Hartlepool 20th worst!). But there have been lots of memorable moments in the decade since as well.

AGUERO WINS TITLE FOR CITY

I am sure everyone remembers Martin Tyler's wonderful 'Agueroooo. . . !!!' moment in 2012 when the Argentinian scored in the 94th minute against QPR in the final game of the season to give Manchester City the Premier League title and, almost as importantly to some, deny their rivals, Manchester United. That was part of Sky Sports' live coverage. But with so many issues at stake, the *Soccer Saturday* gang were also having to focus on promotion, top four and relegation issues. City against QPR was the game Paul Merson was covering and with 55 minutes gone and the scores level, it exploded. Joey Barton elbowed Carlos Tevez and in the melee that followed, kicked Sergio Aguero, tried to headbutt Vincent Kompany and had to be held back from reaching Mario Balotelli. Merse was in full flow.

'Jeff, it's like a scene from *Platoon* out there, there are bodies everywhere!' he shouted.

'There is barely a player on the field he hasn't assaulted,' I added.

Later Barton tweeted that he still didn't think it was a red card. The FA disagreed and gave him a 12-game ban.

With 90 minutes up on the clock and QPR leading 2–1, it looked as though the 10 men would still deny City the title. Edin Dzeko equalised in the 90th minute but that would not be enough and the game was into the dying seconds. I was in the middle of describing United's preparations to lift the trophy – their game had finished early and we were on shots of Sir Alex and Wayne Rooney – when City scored again. Merse exploded, 'It's gone mad!' his mic flying off. 'Roberto Mancini is on the pitch, running around. They are all cuddling each other – they're giving each other love bites and everything!'

It wasn't the sort of thing you would normally have heard on a football commentary but it was a brilliant, colourful, laugh out loud one-line description which summed up perfectly the mayhem on the pitch after the most dramatic climax to a season in Premier League history. In top-flight terms, it is probably matched only by Arsenal going to Liverpool in the final game of the season in 1989 needing to win by two clear goals to lift the title. Anything less and Liverpool would be Champions. They had been woefully out of form and Liverpool were odds-on to prevail. But goals from Alan Smith, and Michael Thomas in injury-time, gave Arsenal the victory they needed. Paul Merson wasn't commentating on that one. He was playing for the Gunners.

WATFORD SCORE FROM LEICESTER PENALTY

A year after City lifted the Premier League title, Watford won a place in the Championship play-off final in the most extraordinary fashion. Again the *Soccer Saturday* team were working overtime on a Special.

Leicester City went to Vicarage Road leading 1–0 from the first leg, but as the second leg headed towards full-time, Watford led 2–1 which meant the scores were level on aggregate. The fourth official had signalled four minutes of added time, but 96 minutes had been played when ref Michael Oliver decided that Anthony Knockaert had been fouled inside the area. It was a penalty to Leicester. If City scored they would be in the play-off final with a glorious chance of returning to the top division. The home fans could not bear to look. Johnny Phillips was our reporter and we crossed to him live.

'Here we go. . .' said Johnny, little knowing the goal that was about to be scored would not be for Leicester.

'Oh, he's saved it, a brilliant save, a fantastic save, a double save from Almunia!' But Johnny was aware that something incredible was happening as he looked down at his monitor. 'Now Watford are breaking, they're bursting forward, they're going to cross it . . .' his voice going into full falsetto mode now, his eyes on stalks. 'They've crossed it . . . AND THEY'VE SCORED!' yelled Johnny, unconsciously leaping in the air as the ball went in, with yellow and red flares exploding around him. 'Oh my god, I just do not believe what I have just seen, Deeney has scored for Watford. Watford have scored from a Leicester penalty!'

Later, Johnny explained how he was totally emotionally drained, not due to support or sympathy for one side or the other, but because of the 'utterly obscene amount of drama packed into those few seconds at the end of the game'. His description had been electrifying and became an internet sensation. No doubt about it, the best 30 seconds of work he has ever done!

FIRE

It was January 2015 and we were in the build-up to that Saturday's matches when the fire alarm rang loudly around the Sky Sports studios. I had just introduced an interview with Tony Pulis, who had recently been appointed as new manager of West Bromwich Albion.

Within a few seconds we were told we had to leave the building. Being born argumentative, I refused initially, partly because I expected it would be a false alarm, partly because it was freezing outside, but mainly because we had a finely crafted show to present and any delay would screw the timings up badly. But I relented. We left Tony Pulis talking about the job at West Brom and trooped outside into one of the Sky Sports car parks. Twenty-seven minutes later we were still there and the Pulis interview was still playing on a loop, time after time after time. A viewer tweeted to suggest that the authorities should play it to inmates at Guantanamo Bay to make them confess. A bit harsh, I thought.

Eventually we were ushered back in to the *Soccer Saturday* studios. Some of the firemen wanted photos and of course we were happy to oblige. I thought when we got back on air the best way to explain our sudden absence was to have the fire fighters on set. And they were happy to oblige. But even as I posed in one of their bright yellow helmets, I did wonder if somewhere in Isleworth at that moment there might be another fire, or a cat up a tree that needed their urgent help. As they finally went back on duty, I introduced the next item.'

'Now, for those of you who didn't see the whole thing, time to hear from the new manager of West Bromwich Albion, Tony Pulis . . .'

DAVE THOMAS

Dave Thomas was a footballing hero of mine. When he was at Burnley and Queens Park Rangers I used to love his ability to dribble, no shin pads, socks down by ankles. The more defenders kicked him, the more determined he was to take them on again and beat them. So I was moved when I heard that the man who had terrorised defences was registered blind and was trying to raise funds to help him, and others, afford a blind dog.

Dickie Davies went to his home to meet him in a very emotional interview. Dave was suffering from severe glaucoma and though he could see straight ahead, he had virtually no peripheral vision. He now needed a white stick when walking. He could still play golf, but needed to hit it straight. A slice or hook and he had to rely on his playing partners to tell him where the ball had gone.

Dave was often close to tears during Dickie's interview, not because he was feeling sorry for himself. I think the man who won eight England caps was simply emotional about the fact that people still remembered him and still cared about him. Soon after, Dave got his guide dog Hannah and in years since has maintained his fund-raising efforts on behalf of others. A truly moving feature.

JOSE MOURINHO

Being studio-based on Saturdays, I don't necessarily meet all the Premier League managers. That was the case with Jose Mourinho, until 2016 when I went to Old Trafford with Rachel Riley to speak to the Manchester United manager. Jose could not have been nicer. When we were introduced he welcomed me with, 'Oh, the funny guy from Saturday afternoons' – high praise from the Special One. The interview was gentle and undemanding and everyone went away happy. A year or so later, *Soccer Saturday* producer Ian Condron rang me late on a Friday evening.

'I've got some good news,' he said. 'You are going to interview Jose live on the show tomorrow.'

'Fantastic,' I replied. 'What a coup!'

Then he told me the truth – that Jose didn't, for one reason or another, want to fulfil his obligation to provide a sit-down interview with Sky prior to the *Super Sunday* game with Chelsea. He only agreed to speak to me after the Premier League intervened and warned him of the consequences.

'Not so fantastic then!' I said. I suspected this could be awkward and it was.

Early in the show the next day, I saw on one of the off-air monitors a grim-faced Mourinho taking his seat for the interview. I still thought I could win him over during the next few minutes with my charm and friendly banter. I opened with a real soft ball question, asking if he was looking forward to the game against his old club. There was no reaction, just silence. Merse leant over to me and said, 'I don't think he can hear you, Jeff.' But he could and eventually replied, 'Yes,' and the game began. I knew we had been allocated six minutes with the Monosyllabic One and I was determined to use it. Jose was determined to give nothing away. Every answer was 'yes', 'no', 'perhaps', 'good', 'bad', 'fit' or 'unfit'. There was only one chink in his armour. United had a huge fixture backlog and were playing two games a week. The media were full of stories of how tired the players must be. 'Never mind the players, Jose, how tiring is it for the manager?' I asked. There was the briefest of smiles and I thought I had him. 'Tiring,' he said, glum again. It was six minutes of purgatory for me, probably for him, and certainly for the viewers.

Note to self: Get me out of here!

Have I interviewed Jose again? No.

Do I envy the match day reporters who have to? No.

Was he my most difficult interviewee? Yes.

Was I surprised when he became a Sky pundit? Very.

FORT WILLIAM

When I had the idea to visit Britain's worst football club for a *Soccer Saturday* feature, I knew there was only one man for the job. Johnny Phillips had visited the Scilly Isles, who boast the smallest league in the world with just two teams. He had interviewed the bird-loving Torquay chairman in a cage full of macaws. He'd done a feature on a team in the Isle of Arran and followed Chris Kamara and Paul Merson to mid-Wales as they tried to revive the fortunes of struggling Welshpool Town. He is a sort of footballing Bill Bryson.

When they caught my eye, Fort William had not won a game for nearly two years. They were bottom of the Highland League on minus seven points. They had drawn two matches, but also had nine points deducted for fielding ineligible players. They were a team of part-timers getting around £20 a week to play against full-time professionals. Johnny planned the feature for 7 April, when they were at home to Nairn County. We had been told this was a game they thought they could win, though I am not sure what they based their optimism on. Our plans were almost wrecked in February when Fort William led a game 1–0 at half-time, only for the referee to call it off due to waterlogging. The big day came in April and could not have gone better for us, though it could have gone better for our hosts. The ref got stuck in traffic and arrived 40 minutes late. When he got there he decided there needed to be an inspection before the match could go ahead because of the amount of deer poo on the pitch. I reported the delay on *Soccer Saturday*.

'There's an official on the pitch with a shovel. That brings to mind a phrase. No, I won't go there. Perhaps someone has had a stag party!'

When the game finally did get underway Fort William dreams were shattered. They lost 6–2. Traffic jams and deer poo meant Johnny had missed his flight home and had to spend a night there. But it made for a wonderfully entertaining feature, the sort that *Soccer Saturday* has the time and ability to do.

Fort William finished the season, bottom, still on minus seven points. They did though eventually end their winless run in September 2019 when they beat Clachnacuddin 1–0. They had waited 29 months, 882 days and 74 games for a victory.

MIGUEL ALMIRON

When Newcastle United signed Miguel Almiron for £21 million from the American side Atlanta United, they thought they knew what they were getting – an all-action player who scored goals. They were right in part. The Paraguayan was like a Duracell bunny, keeping going from the first minute to the last. The Toon Army loved him for his effort, but the elusive first goal just would not come. He got into the right positions, had some glorious opportunities but hadn't managed to take any of them. The wait went on through August, September and October. By November, even his biggest fans were beginning to doubt he would ever score. He had played 27 games and the harder he tried, the less he looked like breaking his duck. Despite that he was a popular figure in the Premier League thanks to his effort and his constantly smiling demeanour. Then four days before Christmas he gave the Geordies the moment they had been waiting for and provided my favourite moment of the 2019–20 season.

It was 4.38 pm and the home game against Crystal Palace was petering out into yet another tedious goalless draw for Newcastle when it happened. Paul Merson was in full flow, but I jumped straight in.

'And he has done it. He has done it at last. I am not talking David McGoldrick at Sheffield United. I'm talking about someone who has waited even longer for a goal. He says he dreams of it. He says he will be so happy when he does it – and now he has done it, Phil Thompson.'

'And it has erupted!' exploded Thommo. 'St James' Park has erupted. Andy Carroll lifts him in the air. He should be thanking his manager because he has stuck by him throughout all this. He has tried, he has tried and failed and failed, but now he has scored his goal. It is 1–0 to Newcastle in the 83rd minute. It's from the penalty spot, falling back, left foot, right into the roof of the net. One-nil!' bellowed Thommo, his voice rising to a crescendo. He had delivered his report to a backdrop of delirious, celebrating Newcastle fans. Manager Steve Bruce would say later he had never heard a roar like it as the relieved Almiron peeled off his shirt, threw it high into the air and raced towards the touchline to be engulfed by joyous players and fans. It was a real festive season feelgood moment for everyone bar Palace supporters.

'He has tried his socks off,' I continued, 'and now he has done it. It is going to be a great Christmas in the Almiron household.' It was probably a great Christmas in the Newcastle club shop too. Never mind Santa down the chimney. Up the Toon!

IT'S FOR YOU, JEFF

This is not something I should be proud of. Everyone knows it is totally unprofessional to leave your phone on during a live show, especially when it hasn't even been muted. We were deep into that Saturday's programme when my phone, which was in my briefcase on the floor, began to ring. It was too loud to ignore so I hauled the briefcase onto the desk, pulled out the phone and answered it, live on air. At first I pretended it was my wife, but I could not believe it when the genuine caller answered me. It was Sky Broadband, just checking that I was happy after a recent issue they had helped me with. Now that's what I call service!

STICK TO COUNTDOWN, JEFF

Over the years we have put a lot of time and money into the *Soccer Saturday Christmas Specials*. They have ranged from our own version of *Superstars* (never has a show been more inappropriately titled than our version) to the *Y Factor* where a tearful John Salako, singing, 'Don't Let the Sun Go Down on Me' beat off strong challengers including Clare Tomlinson singing 'Fever',

Rob McCaffrey with 'A Town Called Malice' and Gary Gillespie with 'Ring of Fire'. Before you ask, I didn't sing. I was Simon Cowell. In 2010 and 2012 we staged our own football tournaments in different parts of the country – Southampton and Liverpool – with our panellists acting as coaches to local kids' teams playing in the Soccer Saturday Cup. This time I was Mike Dean, refereeing every game with an iron fist and a flourish, or so I thought. But as we handed out the awards at the end of the first tournament at the Silverlake Stadium, home of Eastleigh FC, I was brought down to earth. As the captain of the winning team Baddesley Park got his medal, he leaned in and said, 'Do us all a favour, Jeff. Stick to *Countdown*.' And his team had won!

THE SMALLEST LEAGUE IN THE WORLD

Johnny Phillips took the two-and-a-half-hour boat trip from Cornwall to the Scilly Isles to watch the smallest football league in the world (I told you he was Bill Bryson). There are just two teams, Woolpack Wanderers and Garrison Gunners who play each other at Garrison Field on St Mary's every single week of the season. Not only that, but they have two cup competitions as well, one of which is over two legs. If it gets repetitive for the players, pity the referee Phil Charnock, who used to ref in England. He takes charge of every single game. When Johnny filmed his report in October, there was at least a large crowd. Most of them were birdwatchers who had just stumbled upon the game. Unfortunately, they all had their backs turned when Wanderers took a 2–1 lead as someone had spotted an Osprey. And they missed the next goal too as a Little Bunting made a rare appearance. But the birders have helped the Scilly Isles sides break the monotony of their two-team season by putting together a football team of their own to play a friendly every year.

And no, the team's not called Chirpy Chirpy Cheep Cheep.

8

BLACKMAIL

The first letter arrived at my home address early in December of 2017. It was marked 'Strictly Private and Confidential' on both the front and back of the envelope and had been sent from Romford in Essex. It was unusual for pieces of fan mail to come direct to my home, but it had happened on the odd occasion. But this was not fan mail. Not even hate mail. This was blackmail.

At the top of the single sheet of A4, in red letters, was typed a warning. 'It is vitally important only Mr Stelling himself reads this. Failure to ensure Mr Stelling receives this and reads it himself may damage his career and reputation.' This would of course have guaranteed that anyone other than me opening the letter would have read every word that it contained. This is what they would have seen.

Dear Mr Stelling,

We are a highly discreet organization that supplies support, recompense and closure for victims of sexual assault or abuse – often occurring many years prior.

As you can imagine I nearly choked on my Frosties!

One of our clients is making a claim that against you for a serious sexual assault some years ago. Her story and evidence is very detailed and very convincing to me and I would suggest it would be similarly convincing to the authorities or the press. Our client still suffers mental trauma in relation to this incident and has been put in touch with us in order to seek the aforementioned recompense and closure in order to finally move on. Our client however under our advice does not wish to cause damage to your career or to your reputation as she considers that the assault, although very serious in nature, was quite possibly a one-off aberration on your part. For now our client will, on our advice, remain anonymous although we are very aware that the incident mentioned herein will very likely suggest who the client is.

Due to the emotional difficulties that the client has faced since the assault she has never managed to pursue a meaningful career or family life and I suggest the best way to give resolution for the client would be by means of financial recompense. The amount we have suggested to our client as suitable compensation is £50,000. This would enable our client to rebuild her life and take it in the direction she had always hoped.

Our client, also under our advisement is determined that you cannot ignore this matter and simply walk away. Therefore, should you choose not to settle this matter financially the details of you case will be released via a number of news agencies and online resources. The story, once release, cannot be unreleased. In the current political and social environment we feel sure you will understand that this will have lasting damage to your career, your reputation and your personal life. This would in turn almost certainly hurt you more than the modest financial settlement we are seeking.

We are keen to resolve this matter at the earliest opportunity. To that end we have set a 96 hour (4 day) deadline for you to respond. At the end of that period we will commence the process of releasing the files. Our client has also authorized us to negotiate a reduced settlement if, and only if, you respond within 48 hours.

Once we have received a response from you we will maintain the upmost discretion for both you and for our client. An unregistered and untraceable phone

number has been established for communication. To
initiate contact simply text the word 'OCTAVIAN' to
[phone number]. You will then be advised of the next
steps. It is important to note again that after 4 days
the phone number will be discarded and you will
no longer be able to contact us. For your complete
discretion I would suggest that you act for yourself in
this matter and not through a representative. Once we
have arranged and completed settlement our client will
disappear and you will receive no further contact or
threat of action from her or us.

There is a point I need to clarify here. On some
previous cases gentlemen in a similar position to
yourself have though this was some kind of ruse or
the work of a crackpot. Some have simply ignored
it, others have brought it to the attention of various
authorities. The key point here is that in most cases
this mistake has led to them refusing to settle with us
and ultimately to the files being released and causing
themselves far greater difficulties for themselves,
financially and otherwise, than if they had taken it
seriously and settled. You are of course free to act
however you choose. You may of course choose to refer
this letter to any authority. Others have previously
referred these matters to lawyers, police, agents,
employers etc but please bear in mind though that

once you refer this matter, even if you are offered support and protection, you will lose control of how this plays out. We will simply cease contact. The files will still be released and with the social environment as it is right now it is almost certain that your position would become unviable and your will suffer considerable consequential damage. This will provide our client with a different form of redress.

I will repeat. Our client does not wish to damage your career or your reputation but is fully prepared to do so through us should you no take this opportunity to make financial redress now. You have a very short window in which to take that opportunity.

Mr Stelling you have 96 hours in total (or 48 hours if you want us to offer you a reduced settlement).

So there it was. Just like a parking fine. If I paid quickly I would get it at half price!

The letter was littered with grammatical and spelling errors (I have left them all in the text) but then there was no reason that any half-decent blackmailer would have A level English. Of course I knew I had nothing to be concerned about, but receiving something like this was still extremely unpleasant. I showed it to my wife and we both felt the best thing to do was ignore it. But I kept it from my kids and even from my work colleagues.

But I did wonder whether this was something that the blackmailers would persevere with in the hope that they would wear me down. Of course, it was worrying too that they had my home address.

It was also a concern for my wife, who does not enjoy public attention of any sort and certainly not this type. She did not even ask if there was any hint of truth in the letter though, and I was grateful for her total belief in me.

I understand that if you are in any way, shape or form a public figure then you are always vulnerable to a chancer or crackpot with a get-rich-quick scheme. If it becomes public, then of course there is always the danger that some people will believe it. In some people's eyes, there is no smoke without fire, is there?

It had happened to me in my early days in broadcasting when police turned up at Radio Tees, where I was working as a sports presenter, as someone reckoned my voice resembled that of the Yorkshire Ripper, on the 'I'm Jack' tapes. The most worrying thing about this was that if they were right and I did sound like the Ripper, what chance did I have of making a career in radio or television? It was the good cop, bad cop routine that you have seen so often on TV. The first told me what a big fan of my show he was before the second jumped in to ask where I had been on a string of nights when the serial killer had struck. Believe me, it is not easy to remember where you were on a particular day two or three years previously! And what started as a bit of a laugh had now become altogether more serious. Thankfully on a couple of the dates, I could recall being with friends or out at dinner, though even then my alibis were checked out by the police. They even rang my friends and checked reservations. The local papers got hold of the story and ran it with an accompanying photo that to be honest made me look like a serial killer!

The 48-hour deadline in the blackmail letter passed and then the 96-hour time limit. And I heard nothing more. Until just before Christmas when another letter arrived at my home, this time marked 'Private and Urgent'. It was more formally addressed to R J Stelling this time (the first letter was sent using the more friendly Jeff Stelling). I knew straightaway this came from the same source as previous letter. The writing on the envelope was the same and the Romford postmark was the same. Ironically 'Merry Christmas' was stamped across it in large black letters.

The first letter had been typed. This was handwritten, all in block capitals. Perhaps the author thought the more personal touch would have a greater effect. There were no pleasantries this time, no 'Dear Sir'. It got straight down to the nitty gritty.

We sent you a letter recently concerning serous allegations against you by our client. We have not heard from you since, suggesting either that you are not taking this seriously or you are under the mistaken assumption that bringing this to someones attention will prevent us acting.

So for the avoidance of doubt our campaign teams in China and Russia are readying the files right now for release across the internet. Other files will be sent to interested parties (employers, colleagues, family, press etc). These people are very good at what they do and very thorough and once unleashed they will hit you very very hard.

Ignoring this, reporting this or bringing in lawyers will not change anything. The files WILL absolutely be released unless you settle with us.

Right now you still have a way out. You still have control over how this plays out. You settle for a relatively small fee and all this goes away. We go away, never to be seen or heard from again.

To that end my employers have given me permission to offer you one last chance to settle at the discounted fee before we trigger the release. Your only chance to do this is to text your code word to [*phone number*] AND [*phone number*] now. If I haven't heard of you by Wednesday 20th December I will have to assume that you have declined and I won't be able to stop the release.

Remember only text – don't call – instructions will then follow.

Do not concern yourself by what is in the files, where it came from or even if it is genuine. All you need to know is it has the power to ruin your career and your life.

Octavian

Now clearly this had been delayed in the Christmas post, as that day it was already 20 December! Increasingly though, this was like being in a real-life episode of *Inspector Morse*. I expected John Thaw to turn up on my doorstep in his Jaguar Mark 2 any day. I decided it was time to do something about it. I approached Barney Francis, the Managing Director of Sky Sports, and told him exactly what was happening. He was very supportive and set about using the TV station's resources to investigate. The press office rang contacts at Scotland Yard to ask about letters, obviously in confidence. They discovered that a number of similar letters had been sent to a handful of other celebrities and were clearly from the same source. They advised me to ignore them, though if I was concerned about adverse publicity I could try and obtain a gagging order to stop the press publishing names. That was something I didn't consider as I had absolutely nothing to hide.

A few days later though a story ran in a number of national newspapers, saying that a celebrity who was one of a number of people involved in a blackmail plot, had in fact obtained a gagging order to stop their name being released. I never found out who took the legal action.

For weeks – months I suppose – I wondered if I would receive a third letter. After all, as far as I was aware there had been no arrests. I was a little surprised that at no time did the police try and speak to me personally. I never heard from the blackmailers again. But even though I knew I was innocent of any crime, it was a most unsettling time.

And I bet you were all thinking this book was going to be a laugh-out-loud, rib-tickling, family-friendly read. That Christmas, the joke was obviously on me!

9

MONEY MATTERS

Not every letter asking for money is blackmail.

Dear Jeff,

    I doubt this letter will reach you but I have nothing to lose I guess. I am a very proud man so writing this letter has been very difficult for me. I have made a few mistakes in my life when I was younger and have never been able to start on a clear level financially since the age of 18. I have never been in trouble with the police, I don't drink, I don't smoke and I don't do drugs of any kind. There was a period of my life when I was unable to work, which took away 8 good years. Apart from this period I have always worked hard and always had a job including now providing for my girlfriend and baby.

    All that I am asking is that some of my footballing

heroes can make a contribution to me in the hope that I can clear my spiralling debts and get back on an even keel. I don't want much out of life and I don't have a mortgage. I just want a fresh start and to buy my 72 year old mum a nice gift as a thank you for all the things she has done for me over the years. Anything you can do for me will make me eternally grateful and I will be forever in your debt. I am using the very last of my savings to pay for the stamps on these letters. I am not doing this as an internet stunt or for publicity of any kind. That's the last thing I would want so please believe me when I say I am genuine.

I know I am clutching at straws and may sound like a Nigerian banking scam, but I am pleading 100 per cent with you. Here are my bank details

[account details]

I have included my address on the off chance you would prefer to send me something through the post.

Kind regards

Don't call me callous. I did send something through the post – the price of the stamp. The problem is that this did sound like a Nigerian banking scam and you do look at letters like this cynically (he has always had a job and still does, has no mortgage, but can barely afford a stamp!) because in one guise or another, I receive so many. Some clearly believe that flattery gets you every-where.

> Dear Mr Stelling,
> I do hope that this letter finds you well and safe. First and foremost I would like to thank you for all the work you do for different charities and other causes. Thank you so much too for the Soccer Saturday programme which I admit is my favourite programme on Sky Sports News.
> I am kindly looking for help in terms of £20,000 to assist me with a few things.

Well, at least he didn't beat about the bush. There was a phone number for him to explain further why he wanted the money, before the letter's conclusion.

> I will be more than grateful if my request is put into your consideration and I wish Hartlepool all the best.

Of course, you can always lay the flattery on with a trowel.

> Dear Jeff,
> Firstly I would like congratulate you and your colleagues on the terrific show and entertainment that you host on Saturdays and sometimes midweek. I have

always been a really big fan of yours. The verve and humour with which you present is also to be admired. I find your energy and enthusiasm for your team to be admired too. I also feel the way you present, you really connect with your listeners. I think sometimes it is like a personal football show in my lounge presented by my best mate. It does really come over that fantastically well . . .

Now I have condensed this as the letter runs for four full pages of A4!

. . . I have a problem that I hope you can help me with Jeff. Put simply my dad is retiring and putting the family hotel business up for sale. After some stressful negotiation I have agreed to buy the business from him early next year. After agreeing the price and speaking with my bank about a loan, I now find myself in the stressful position of being £10,000 short for my deposit/ solicitors fees/stamp duty. I know you are not a bank or loan company Jeff but you seem such an amazing chap on TV that I thought, maybe, just maybe you could help. If you could loan me the £10,000, I would pay you back at the first opportunity.

Not the usual fan mail, I guess, but thank you for taking the time to read this. If you could help I would be forever in your debt.

Which, of course, is precisely what I would be worried about. I am afraid I wasn't such an amazing chap and didn't respond. I actually am convinced that the letter was genuine and that the writer was in need of help to buy his dad's business, but it was unlikely to come from me, someone he had never met or even spoken to. Now when I get a letter which starts with, 'Dear Jeff, you are the greatest . . .' I stop reading (okay, maybe not quite straightaway if I am honest) and pop it straight into the bin. It makes me think, if I get so many requests for money, how many does the Bank of Antandec get?

Online now, I get dozens of requests for help from football teams desperate for funding, from charities desperate for auction items and from people wanting me to turn up (but not play, thankfully) at fund-raising games. I don't blame anyone for asking. After all, my club Hartlepool did just that, appealing for help when we were in serious financial trouble.

Often requests are not for money, just help. I received a letter from someone whose son was in hospital in Coventry and could I pop in and visit him to cheer him up!

Of course, it costs nothing to give up our time and sometimes the rewards for doing that are immense. Years ago I responded to a plea for help from the parents of Alice Skinner, a three-year-old Hartlepool girl, who had been born without properly formed kidneys. Alice had needed six operations before her first birthday and spent 10 hours a day on a dialysis machine. Her family were staging a fund raiser but had been let down at very short notice by their star guests. I flew to the Northeast and persuaded former Man United, Leeds and Middlesbrough star Gordon McQueen to join me. Nell McAndrew, who had no connection with the town or the girl, travelled up from Leeds. It ended up being a terrific evening.

My reward came 14 years later when I received a letter from a now not-so-little Alice's mum.

Dear Jeff,

I hope this letter finds you well. I am not sure if you can remember when you attended a Charity do at the Staincliffe Hotel for my daughter Alice Skinner. I will always remember how you flew up to help us out. I have never ever forgotten your generosity and regularly tell people about it.

Fast forward to 2018 and in March Alice will be 17 and now at college. In April, she will celebrate her 10 year kidney transplant anniversary. There have been many ups and downs over the years but she is a very determined young lady who I am very proud of.

Alice attends the British Transplant Games every

year, taking part in sports and celebrating life. She has won at least one medal every year since her transplant.

I congratulate you on your successful career, the amazing kindness you showed us at the original charity event and also the way you keep Hartlepool on the map.

Yours Sincerely,

Nicola Frankland (Alice's mum)

It is a letter I treasure. Doing the right thing sometimes brings rewards that money can't buy.

10

CHAMPIONS LEAGUE

Even the complimentary correspondence had to be put on the back burner when the phone rang at home one afternoon.

The call was from my MD, Barney Francis. 'Jeff, would you be willing to take on our Champions League coverage? It will mean a lot of travel to the likes of Barcelona and Milan.' It was the sort of question that required a full nanosecond of careful thought before answering.

The request came in the aftermath of Richard Keys and Andy Gray leaving the company in January 2011. For me, this was the dream job and it had a dream start.

SAN SIRO

A month or so later Spurs were at the San Siro to face AC Milan in the first leg of the last 16. It was my first game as presenter and would be one of the most memorable and dramatic of my five years covering the competition. We had dinner with Harry Redknapp, then Tottenham manager, the night before the game and he was under no illusions about the size of the task.

On a stormy night, deafening claps of thunder rumbling round the San Siro added to the atmosphere as the teams came out to the Champions League anthem. There was an almost operatic quality to the setting. The home crowd was loud, expectant and hostile. I was with Jamie Redknapp in our outdoor presentation area, set back from the pitch but no more than 25 yards from the dugouts. We were close enough for Harry to hear Jamie's shouts.

Tottenham defended for their lives against the Serie A leaders in what was a brutal contest. And then came a moment of high drama. After 80 minutes, totally against the run of play, Peter Crouch swept home the only goal of the game. The last 10 minutes were sheer bedlam as Zlatan Ibrahimovic had a goal disallowed and Spurs assistant manager Joe Jordan was headbutted by Gennaro Gattuso. On the final whistle Jamie yelled at his dad to come to our presentation position for an interview and to the fury of UEFA officials who wanted him for the official press conference, he did. It was great TV as father and son celebrated live on Sky moments after one of the team's greatest ever victories. Later, we celebrated with Harry and the Spurs management team, my first European night ending with a kiss from Joe Jordan!

ALLIANZ ARENA

In May of the following year Harry was with us again, this time in Munich for the final between Bayern and Chelsea at the Allianz Arena. Tottenham had finished fourth in the Premier League, five points clear of Chelsea and would qualify for the following season's Champions League unless their London rivals could win on Bayern's home ground. Though the Germans were red hot favourites, Chelsea had already shown in the tournament that nothing is impossible. In the second leg of the semi-final in Barcelona, they were down to 10 men after John Terry's sending off and behind on aggregate at half-time. Then came one of the most astonishing 45 minutes I have ever witnessed as Ramires put Chelsea ahead on away goals, Lionel Messi missed a penalty which would surely have won the game for the home team before Fernando Torres ran the length of the pitch to seal an incredible Chelsea victory in injury time.

But after finishing sixth in the Premier League, the only way Chelsea could qualify for the following season's competition was by winning the final in Germany which would eliminate Spurs.

Harry was there on a watching brief, hoping to see his club's entry into next season's competition rubber stamped. We had invited him into the studio to watch the game – after all, Jamie was on the commentary team again. Even though the German side totally dominated, Harry was nervous. He was convinced that Spurs Chairman Daniel Levy would sack him if they failed to qualify – even under these extraordinary circumstances. Then Thomas Mueller scored seven minutes from time and he relaxed a little. Up to that point Chelsea hadn't managed a shot on target. But with two minutes left, Didier Drogba equalised, and after a goalless extra 30 minutes, he rolled in the winning penalty in the shootout. Poor Harry was ashen. I felt desperately sorry for him as ex-Chelsea man Ruud Gullit celebrated wildly in front of him. Harry then faced a walk past thousands of celebrating Chelsea fans who taunted him unmercifully as he left the ground.

On the flight home the following day, Harry was inconsolable and convinced he would lose his job. We all tried to reassure him that wouldn't be the case. After all, his side had finished in the top four on merit. There was nothing that he could do about the unlikely events in Munich.

A month later, Daniel Levy sacked Harry.

SAN PAOLO STADIUM

I had seen a lot of Chelsea in Europe that season including on my first-ever trip to Naples. It's a frightening city, with its dark, narrow streets and reputation as home of the Camorra organisation. Napoli's home ground, the San Paolo Stadium, is as intimidating as any venue in Europe. Sky's policy was to have everyone at the location of an overseas game the day before, which meant we had a night to spend in the city. Gianfranco Zola had arranged to meet us at his favourite restaurant so we jumped into a taxi to get there. Eventually, the driver pulled up in a gloomy side street and pointed down an unlit alleyway. None of us – not even hardman Graeme Souness – was getting out and walking down that alleyway. We insisted that the taxi driver first made sure it was safe and then escorted us to the trattoria door!

The following day we ran the gauntlet of Napoli fans throwing bottles filled with urine into the TV compound. Travelling Chelsea fans were effectively in a cage for their own safety, with netting above their heads to stop the home fans hurling anything down on them. The notorious Curva Nord started to fill up hours before kick-off with the early arrivals lighting fires on the terraces. I wasn't sure why any Chelsea fan would want to be there. And they were probably wondering the same thing themselves by the end. Under-pressure Chelsea manager Andre Vilas Boas decided to leave Frank Lampard, Ashley Cole, Michael Essien and Fernando Torres on the bench. With John Terry already out injured, it looked like footballing suicide and so it proved. Chelsea lost 3–1 and the Portuguese was sacked before the second leg.

NOU CAMP

My favourite city to visit was undoubtedly Barcelona. I loved its Mediterranean feel, great restaurants and the fact that the Nou Camp is so centrally positioned that you could walk to the stadium from the hotel. The football wasn't bad either. In 2015, we went there to see if Manchester City could overturn a first-leg deficit. It wasn't to be. Lionel Messi was at his majestic best, mesmerising City with his passing and dribbling. I was hypnotised by Messi. Often during games I found myself just watching him. Often he would simply stand still, but his head would swivel constantly so he was aware of where every other player was at all times. As Matt Le Tissier says, sometimes running is overrated! City just could not cope with him and it turned out to be a fairly routine passage through to the quarter-finals for Barça.

The match was played on my birthday and the plan was that a group of us including Thierry Henry, Jamie Redknapp, Graeme Souness and the producer Gary Hughes would go to our favourite restaurant, a wonderful, atmospheric place called Botafumeiro. I had to stay in the studio for a few minutes to record a new beginning and end for repeats of the game to be shown later and arranged to meet everyone outside. When I'd finished, I left with floor manager Brett Smart, only to find there was no-one else in sight. They weren't answering their phones. They had all disappeared. I had the hump at being left behind, so Brett and I headed back to the hotel. When the guys did telephone from the restaurant, I dug my heels in and refused to join them. It was late and I had an early start.

The following morning at around 6 am I was checking out of the hotel when a weary looking Thierry Henry, holding a carrier bag, tapped me on the shoulder. Inside the bag was Lionel Messi's autographed shirt – not a replica but the one he had actually worn in the game the previous night. After the match, Thierry had taken the others into the Barcelona dressing room to ask Messi for the shirt as my birthday present. They had hoped to give it to me at Botafumeiro. I was desperately embarrassed. I was working with some footballing legends, but it was me who had behaved like a prima donna. The shirt is framed and takes pride of place at my home.

WESTFALENSTADION

Barcelona was my favourite city but the Westfalen-stadion, home of Borussia Dortmund, is my favourite ground. My first visit there was for the first leg of their semi-final against Real Madrid in 2013. The atmosphere was the best I have ever experienced at a football ground. Outside, stall after stall sold beer and bratwurst, but there was no hint of trouble. Inside, everyone was swathed in yellow and black. It seemed like a condition of entry. Our presentation position was on a platform literally in the centre of the crowd, surrounded by Dort-mund fans. I could see Graeme Souness, who has played in many of the world's great arenas, looking round in amazement. If it was loud at the start, you could not hear yourself think 20 minutes into the second half when Robert Lewandowski scored his and Dortmund's fourth goal of the night. A Madrid team including Sergio Ramos, Luca Modric, Xabi Alonso, Gonzalo Higuain and Cristiano Ronaldo had been demolished. Dortmund lost to Bayern Munich in the final at Wembley, but I had fallen in love with their fans and their ground.

OTHER VENUES

Of course, it wasn't always glamorous. Sky took a late decision to send us to the second leg of the 2014–15 semi-final between Real Madrid and Juventus. But there was no studio space left at the Bernabeu, so while we could broadcast from pitchside before the game, at half-time and at the end, when Alvaro Morata scored the goal that took the Italians to the final, we were huddled in a groundsman's storage cupboard under the main stand watching on TV.

When there was no room for a studio at the Estadio da Luz for Chelsea's game at Benfica in 2012 we watched from the stands, sitting among the home fans before rushing to the pitch for half-time and full-time.

On another occasion, Glenn Hoddle and I were left eating crisps and drinking '1664' at midnight in one of Europe's greatest cities, Paris. Chelsea had played PSG and afterwards the Sky team was heading for a pre-arranged rendezvous with former England cricketer Kevin Pietersen. But the traffic was appalling and it was late by the time we arrived. We were greeted with a wall of thumping music as we entered what seemed more like a nightclub than a restaurant. Glenn and I and floor manager Brett Smart decided we would try and find somewhere else. But this must have been the quietest arrondissement in the city. Nothing was open. We ended up being the only customers sitting outside a café which was about to close. The patron brought us as many beers as the table would hold, closed up the inside and went home! Dinner was half a dozen packets of cheese and onion crisps that Brett had in his backpack, the leftovers of the nibbles provided for the presentation team at the game. Glenn was in great form, entertaining us with stories that ranged from Eileen Drury to leaving Gazza out of his World Cup squad in 1998, but it wasn't quite the great gastronomic experience we had been hoping for.

We only travelled abroad when the competition reached the knockout phase. For group matches, we stayed at Sky's studios in Isleworth with a three-strong panel. These shows usually started at 6 pm with a monster hour and three quarters build-up to the main game. You needed your team of pundits to be well prepared. This wasn't always the case. I remember Ruud Gullit turning up one day as the titles were rolling. As he sat down, he asked what the game was. When I told him, he asked who was at home! Karl-Heinz Riedle was a great guest when it came to talking about his old club Liverpool. When it came to talking about their opposition, however, he looked blank and said, 'I am sorry, I know nothing about them.' Honesty is not always the best policy in broadcasting, Karl-Heinz!

I always enjoyed it when Graeme Souness was on the panel. We first met when he was a player at Middlesbrough in the 1970s and even though we didn't see each other for years, we quickly got on well again. He was always opinionated and I think secretly liked being taken on in debates. In 2014, when Manchester City had started their Champions League campaign sluggishly, Graeme defended them, by pointing out that a lot of their players were still tired after the World Cup in Brazil.

'But Graeme, why is it that Barcelona's players and Real Madrid's players and Bayern Munich's players don't seem to be still tired from the World Cup? They are all top of their groups,' I said in mischief. I had the Godfather in trouble and he knew it. In the next commercial break, he asked me what time the show ended. Eleven o'clock, I told him. 'I'll have you before then, you bastard,' he said.

I hosted five Champions League finals live from the grounds. As well as Chelsea's win in Munich against Bayern, I saw Barcelona twice lift the trophy by beating

Manchester United and Juventus. I was at Wembley when Bayern won the all-German encounter against Borussia Dortmund. But my favourite final was in the Estadio da Luz in 2014 when the two Madrid sides, Real and Atletico went head to head. But I almost missed it! I had taken my family with me to Lisbon and we enjoyed the vibrant atmosphere in the city created by the supporters of the two sides. But I was in the stadium rehearsing by early afternoon. When my sons arrived at the ground at around six in the evening, I left the studio and headed out of the stand to meet them and show them where they would be sitting. But when it came to getting back to the studio, a security guard would not let me through. I had the wrong pass!

I called the production manager, who came and tried to reason with the guard, but he would not be budged. There was now only half an hour until we were on the air. I was hot and flustered and most importantly still unable to get back to the studio. The production manager asked if her pass was the right one. When she was told it was, she simply swapped hers with mine right in front of the security guard's eyes. He watched what was happening and then waved me through. So it was not okay to get in using the wrong pass, but it was okay using the correct pass even if it belonged to someone else! The game itself was full of drama with Atletico holding onto a first-half lead until the 93rd minute when Sergio Ramos headed an equaliser for their more illustrious neighbours. Atletico were a spent force. Gareth Bale put Real in front in extra-time and they ran out 4–1 winners. Diego Simeone, the Atletico manager, was sent off in the closing moments of an enthralling encounter. I was glad I had managed to get inside to watch it!

It was the Champions League that ended my time at *Countdown*. Channel 4 controller Helen Warner and producer Damian Eadie had been brilliant in helping juggle things around for me. But we recorded five shows a day in three-day blocks at the Manchester studios. My schedule was making it difficult for them as well as me. I realised something had to give in a week where I flew to Milan on Monday for a Tuesday night match. I was on the return flight at 6 am on Wednesday. A car was waiting for me at Heathrow to whisk me to Manchester so we could start recording our 15 shows from 1 o'clock in the afternoon. I caught a train back to Euston at 5 o'clock on the Friday evening so I could start my prep for *Soccer Saturday*, worked until 2 am at my hotel and was at Sky by 6 am to continue catching up. By the time I had arrived home in Winchester at 8.30 pm, I knew I would have to give up either *Countdown* or Sky. It was no contest! Damian suggested we could record more shows each day and so I would have to be in Manchester less often. But I knew people were exhausted after five shows. It would not be fair on anyone. I was sad to leave Rachel Riley, Susie Dent and the rest of the *Countdown* team behind, but I knew it was the right thing to do, even though I had loved following in the prestigious footsteps of Richard Whiteley, Des O'Connor and Des Lynam.

The former right-hand man to Sir Alan Sugar on *The Apprentice*, Nick Hewer, took my place and in doing so provided an open goal for the press. What was the headline in every newspaper the following day? 'YOU'RE HIRED!'

11

MARATHON MAN

START

Dear Jeff,

I am one of those very silly people who have ·
terminal prostate cancer because they didn't get it
checked out in time. I believe that your efforts will have
saved thousands from that fate.

Please let me take you back to 3 March 1962, exactly
55 years ago.

An awful day at Wrexham with snow and hail,
much more a winter's day than spring. I had travelled
to the ground early to collect autographs and as you can
see managed 7 from that days opposition, Hartlepools
United. Three hours later we were celebrating with a
Tizer and a bag of chips, Wrexham's biggest ever
league victory 10–1 (You were lucky to get one!)

I am giving away all my 60 years of football collections and would like to give this to you (I don't know if you are a collector but you may be.)

Good luck, Yours Sincerely,

Peter Tudor

Enclosed was the autographed programme from the game.

It is fair to say that when I set off on the first of my 29 walking marathons to raise awareness of prostate cancer, I did not realise what I was letting myself in for. True, before I had taken a step I had been warned that walking 26.2 miles was as tough as running 26.2 miles, but I didn't believe that for a moment. I'd run eight marathons and nothing could be as tough. Or so I thought.

It didn't help that on the first batch of walks – the 'March to the Arch' from Hartlepool to Wembley – the route appeared to have been mapped out by Ant Middleton and the *SAS: Who Dares Wins* team. We battled through waist-high grass, clambered over stiles and fences, limped along cobbled stretches of walkways, were chased from a field by an angry farmer and abseiled down rock faces. Okay, I am exaggerating about the abseiling. But a lot of those walking were over 60 and suffering from prostate cancer. We were trying to help save them, not kill them off.

But we certainly didn't know what we were facing as I set off on that bright and breezy morning with Hartlepool United chief executive Russ Green and a group that included ex-England, Man U and Chelsea star Ray Wilkins, ex-Liverpool and Middlesbrough striker Craig Hignett and Alastair Campbell, formerly political aide to Tony Blair and still a big Burnley fan. Alastair has always supported the walks and on this one told me of a meeting of the Labour hierarchy, who were wrestling over names of people that best reflected the party values. After a number of big names had been put forward, Campbell came out with 'Jeff Stelling'. To which there was a unanimous response of 'Who?'

By halfway on that first day, it was clear this was no walk in the park. I had started in boots with the intention of changing into trainers for the last 10 miles or so. But when the time came, my feet were too swollen to fit into them.

One man with a banner lifted flagging spirits though.

At the time Jack Marriott was scoring lots of goals for Luton, as was Danny Hylton at Oxford (and later Luton). When they both scored during *Soccer Saturday*, as they frequently did, I would say, 'All we need now is a goal from Tommy Travelodge to complete a unique hat trick.'

There on the promenade in late afternoon, not far from our finish point in Marske was a man with a banner proclaiming 'I am Tommy Travelodge'. My feet were red raw and blistered and my 61-year-old body was protesting painfully, but I laughed the rest of the way to the end of the first leg.

Among those wanting to meet us at the end were a couple who waited in the freezing cold night air until everyone else had gone. The lady explained that she had seen us wearing our 'Men of Men' badges on *Soccer Saturday* one day but wasn't aware of what they were. She googled the badge and then went to the Prostate Cancer UK website where she looked at the symptoms of this wretched illness. Her husband had them all. He had since undergone surgery and his prognosis was now good.

'I wanted to thank you,' she said. 'Wearing the badge saved my husband's life.'

The second day's 26.2 miles from York to Leeds became 33 miles as our group of walkers became too spread out and half of us managed to get lost. Even the ever-exuberant Chris Kamara – who was dressed more for a nightclub than a trek, in tight black jeans and pristine white shirt – was quiet by his standards. A group of squaddies walking with us were seriously regretting their four pints each during the hour-long lunch stop. (They told me that during their training for the walk they had spotted a pub, but when they arrived realised there was a wake being held. 'Never mind lads,' said the widow, 'Bert loved the military, come and join us.' So they did. For more than four pints and longer than an hour.)

It was on this leg that I first met Lloyd Pinder, one of the most resilient men who I will ever meet. We chatted about his beloved Sunderland, and his wife, Tina and two daughters aged seven and three. He forgot to mention he had been diagnosed with terminal prostate cancer two months earlier at the age of just 44. His kids, who I met at halfway, knew nothing about their dad's illness. Nor did any of his friends. He and his wife were carrying the burden between them.

Every day I would do a chat with Paul Hawksbee and Andy Jacobs live on talkSPORT. That day I used the time to tell the listeners about the incredible positivity of the man I had just met. Prostate cancer at 44. And a Sunderland fan as well – a real double whammy. But I didn't reveal his name, just told the listeners that his daughters and his friends were all unaware of his illness. That evening Lloyd got a call from his best friend Colin Brierley, who had been listening to talkSPORT.

'Lloyd, have you got something to tell me, mate?' it started.

Lloyd has been with me on many of the walks since. His attitude and determination, his unwillingness to feel sorry for himself, is inspirational. He is one of the main reasons I have now done 29 walking marathons for PCUK.

But just two days in and the walk was already in crisis. Russ – who was doing all ten days with me –and I wanted some guarantees that the 33-mile farce of the previous day would not be repeated. We also wanted to be given some waypoints during the march to give us some idea of how far we had walked and more signifi-cantly how far we still had to go.

Our overnight stay on that second night was at the very welcoming Earl of Doncaster Hotel where I was given the best room in the house, the Love Suite. The centrepiece was a huge double bed. The walls were adorned with bright lipstick-red hearts and sensual photos and ornaments. The following morning our fan-tastic physio, Jo Jennings, a former Olympic high jumper, came into the room to try and massage my aching bones.

'Where do you want me, Jo?' I asked.

'I never thought I would be saying this to Jeff Stelling in the Love Suite of a Doncaster hotel,' she responded, 'but I want you on the bed and quickly!' Of course, she meant she still had to massage Russ Green too and was running short of time.

The morning of Day 3 though was the nadir of the march. We were heading from Doncaster to Scunthorpe, still aching from the extra mileage of the previous days and with the Wembley arch feeling an impossible distance away. Neither Russ nor I thought we could make it. The weather that day was miserable and we were accompanied by the smallest group of walkers of the entire journey. Spirits could not have been any lower.

Then at our halfway stop something of a miracle happened. It was the gift of a god. A cricketing god! And a walking god! Without any announcement, Sir Ian Botham, his wife Kathy, daughter Sarah and his dog had turned up to take part in the second half of the day's walk. They were brilliant with everyone, lifted morale, and turned a terrible day into a good one as he led us into the promised land of Scunthorpe. Beefy's intervention was a real turning point in the walk.

A couple of days later we were on a towpath by the River Trent when Paul Merson unwittingly did his level best to see off some of the very people we were trying to save. It was a glorious, unseasonably warm spring day with the sun beating down. As we walked and talked, Merse fumbled with his sunglasses case and sent it flying into the Trent.

'Oh my god, my designer sunglasses!' shouted Merse. 'They cost me a fortune and they're brand new.'

It was several feet down to the slow-flowing river and immediately one of our number started to strip off, ready to dive in after the designer sunglasses. Not a good idea. We managed to dissuade him and instead a number of people ran ahead, lowered one walker head first towards the water while clutching his ankles, and when the designer sunglasses floated past, he leaned out and with the help of a stick, pulled them in. He was hauled up and triumphantly presented the sunglasses case to a relieved Merse. He opened the case. It was empty. As we looked up at Merse, we realised why. There, sitting on the top of his head were his new designer sunglasses. In the panic to recover the glasses, no-one had bothered to look at the bloke who had spent a fortune on his new shades.

Storm Katie lashed the walkers one day, Russ needed Northampton Town physios to get him to the start on another. But against all odds, Russ and I reached Wembley on Day 10. The problem is you can see the Arch from miles away, but it never seemed to get any closer. Finally we reached Wembley Way, 261 miles covered. The problem was, to complete the 10 marathons we needed to have covered 262 miles. The organisers broke the news that we would have to walk another mile around the stadium before we could go in. It may not sound much – one more mile – but it was like a kid looking through a sweetshop window, but not being allowed in. When finally we walked into the stadium to fireworks, brilliantly lit scoreboards and huge applause, we fell into each other's arms and both said the same thing. Never again.

FINISH

A year later I set off on 15 marathons in 15 days from St James Park, Exeter to St James' Park Newcastle (uphill all the way, according to Paul Merson, looking at a map of the United Kingdom).

The walk was again supported by lots of celebrities including all the *Soccer Saturday* regulars – Matt Le Tissier, Paul Merson, Phil Thompson, Charlie Nicholas, Ian Dowie, Bianca Westwood, Neil Mellor, Kammy and Michelle Owen among them. Regular supporters like Colin Murray and Alastair Campbell dusted off their walking boots again. The giant ex-Wolves keeper Matt Murray did a leg. (I did around 60,000 steps that day – Matt covered the same distance in about 30,000. Life can be so unfair.) And en route we were joined by the likes of Robbie Fowler, Franny Benali, Mark Lawrenson, Danny Mills, Paul Jewell, Ronnie Moore, Andre Marriner, Paul Collingwood, Kevin Sinfield, Phil Clarke, Sean Dyche and a host of others. We even had video messages from luminaries like Stephen Fry.

Over the course of the 15 days, footballing royalty like Gordon Banks, Denis Law, Mike Summerbee and Jimmy Montgomery came out to greet us.

My Sky Sports colleague and prostate cancer sufferer Bill Arthur was there too. I had known Bill for many years and the fact that both he and the brilliant Sky Sports Rugby League presenter Eddie Hemmings were sufferers brought it home to me that everyone knows someone with prostate cancer because it is so widespread. But men, being what they are, have never wanted to talk about it. They never want to go to a doctor. And certainly not if it was about something below the waist. That was the attitude we were trying to change. Many of the people on the walks had loved ones with prostate cancer, had lost people to it or had been diagnosed with the illness themselves.

Kevin Webber was in the last group. Kevin was diagnosed with terminal prostate cancer in 2014 at the age of 49 and given two years to live. Whoever provided that estimate clearly did not understand Kevin Webber. The following year he completed the Brighton and London marathons while undergoing chemotherapy. Since then he has raised hundreds of thousands of pounds entering ultra events all over the world. He took part in the Yukon 6633, a nine-day non-step trek in sub-zero temperatures across the Arctic Circle, where you pull your own sledge, carry your tent and supplies and have wolves for company. The Marathon des Sables, six days across the Sahara, covering around 150 miles, is regarded as the toughest foot race in the world. Kev did it for four years in a row. And when coronavirus caused the cancellation of the 2020 race, Kevin staged his own, covering 3,285 laps of his garden. Carrying his back pack, of course.

He had done all 10 legs of the March to the Arch and was intending to complete all 15 days' walking from Exeter to Newcastle. When a family crisis meant he had to dash home midway through the event, he did what only Kevin Webber could do and ran or walked a marathon each day he was away. I've talked to him many times on the walks and he is driven by his desire to make the most of every day he has left on earth. His mantra is, if you have a bad day, make absolutely sure the next one is a good day.

Day after day you would find him encouraging, cajoling and helping anyone who was struggling in any way he could. 'You are doing this,' he would tell people, 'to save the lives of my two boys.' Powerful motivation for anyone.

I was chuffed to bits when he was named Endurance Fundraiser of the Year 2018 and I was asked to present him with the award. I fail to understand, when sports-people, political lackeys, film stars and those who have made a fortune for just doing their jobs, receive honours, how Kevin Webber has been overlooked. Never mind the MBE or OBE, if there was any justice, by now he would be Sir Kevin.

Funnily enough, I found the 15 marathons in 15 days easier than the 10 in 10 the previous year. It was probably because I knew what to expect. I knew the first 15 or 16 miles or so would be literally like a walk in the park. But then, just as in a running marathon, you hit the wall. Some of my Sky Sports colleagues didn't find it so comfortable. Matt Le Tissier walked one of the early legs from Swindon to Forest Green Rovers with his wife Angela. It was a beautiful day and the walk had gone well, but I thought the organisers had made an error of judgement by including a refreshments stop at a pub four miles from the finish. Tiss made it into the pub. But he never came out. It was left to Angela to uphold the Le Tissier family name as she made it all the way to the finish. The final climb to the finish at the New Lawn by the way made climbing Mount Kilimanjaro, which I had done a few years earlier, look easy. Dale Vince, the Forest Green owner, could do with getting a cable car installed.

Unlike my trek up Kilimanjaro, I had extra food supplies on these walks as my wife would send parcels containing packets of Cadbury Giant Chocolate Buttons, vitamins and Vaseline with lovely encouraging letters from her and my daughter, Olivia. My oldest son Robbie had already walked a leg and Matt would join me on the penultimate leg, which all helped keep my spirits high.

Ex-Liverpool and England star Robbie Fowler was cajoled into joining us on the leg from Chester to Liverpool. He was gutsy in making it all the way to Everton's Goodison Park, the finishing point, despite having been in trouble for the last few miles. He described it later on radio as one of the toughest things he had ever done! I was pleased that a professional athlete had come out and said it in public. It helped make people realise the magnitude of what my fellow walkers, especially those who were ill, were achieving.

We crossed the Pennines in the company of Sean Dyche and made our way through North Yorkshire, with St James' Park, Newcastle ever closer. At one North Yorkshire village an entire primary school class came out with brightly coloured posters they had designed, all with the encouraging message, 'You can do it, Unbelievable Jeff.' I am not sure too many of them knew who this particular Jeff was, but it was lovely to see.

Russ Green, who had stuck with his 'never again' pledge, joined us for the final leg from Durham to Newcastle. Bonkers as it sounds, by now I was really enjoying every 26 miles but incredibly, at the drinks reception at St James' Park, no fewer than three of our walkers passed out. It had been tough. But the 15 marathons were done, 25 in total. In my office I have a framed picture of me crossing the line, being greeted by Ellie, one of the brilliant Prostate Cancer UK team. In the background are Russ Green, Kevin Webber and Lloyd Pinder.

In two walks, we and all those who joined us had raised more than £700,000. Two years later PCUK approached me with an idea for 'Jeff's March to a Million!'

ENCORE

By definition, you have to live until you die. Better to make that life as complete and enjoyable an experience as possible, in case death is shite, which I suspect it will be.

I don't think Irvine Welsh had prostate cancer sufferers in mind when he wrote that in *Trainspotting*, but I suspect it's how Kevin Webber and Lloyd Pinder and a host of others live their lives. I was worried about Lloyd, who wasn't well enough to take part in any day of the third set of marathons.

Chatting to Irvine at the start of the first day on our

March to a Million felt like I was actually in *Trainspotting*. I had never met him before and as we set off from Hampden Park, he was a solitary figure striding out at the front. I hurried to catch up and introduce myself. As an ice-breaker I asked him about his team, Hibs, and their then manager Paul Heckingbottom. His responses used every language in the book – 'colourful' would be to put it mildly. Let's just say, Irvine was a fan of Hibs but not their manager. I get the impression the language he uses in his books is not there specifically to shock, it is just how Irvine would express himself in some of the situations his characters find themselves in. He was a robust walker and did the 26.2 miles with no problem.

There were just four marathons in four days this time, which sounds straightforward enough. What made it less so was that they were in different countries – Scotland, Northern Ireland, Wales and England. I had long wanted to take the walks out of England. After all, we were marching to raise funds for Prostate Cancer UK not Prostate Cancer England! The challenge this presented was physical and logistical. We had to finish each marathon in time to catch a flight or train to the next start point. This meant walking at a decent pace, sacrificing physiotherapy on aching legs, missing out on lovely warm baths at the next hotel and potentially doing without a steak and a beer as a reward for making it through another 26 miles!

Before the start of the first leg, which took us from Hampden to whistle-stop visits to Rangers, Celtic, Hamilton and Motherwell, the receptionist at the Radisson Hotel in Glasgow had presented me with a survival package of chocolate, fruit, biscuits and drinks. It was just the first of many acts of kindness.

By 7.30 am we were ready to go. With one exception. Charlie Nicholas was meant to be on the red-eye from London, but the flight was delayed. While we were setting out on a chilly Glasgow morning, Charlie was in the British Airways lounge at Heathrow living up to his nickname with a glass or two of champagne. By the time he joined us, the ex-Celtic man had missed out on a rare chance to visit Ibrox Park, home of arch rivals, Rangers.

Later that morning we were walking through a glorious wooded area by the riverside. It was a stunning day, the birds were singing and the woods looked beautiful. But one giant oak tree had been defaced by graffiti. Just one. In big white capital letters, it read, 'Charlie Nicholas is a Wanker!' Charlie was happy enough to pose for photos by the tree along with Irvine Welsh. Part of me couldn't help wondering if Irvine had done it!

David Moyes also walked the full distance. I have

always liked David. He is really good company. He was out of work at the time but told me he had turned down offers from Championship clubs, because he still saw himself as a Premier League manager. I took the hint and backed him to be the next Everton manager. Not that long afterwards he was back in charge at West Ham! Remember, the bookies always win.

We made it to the finish in time to dash to Glasgow airport for a late evening flight to Belfast. It had been years since I had been to Belfast and it has certainly changed for the better. Two-time world boxing champion Carl Frampton joined me along with Colin Murray and Ian Dowie. It was here that one of the greatest acts of generosity happened.

Our route took us past Harland and Wolff, the shipyard where the Titanic was built. It once employed 30,000 workers but now only 125 remained. They too were soon to lose their jobs with the famous yard about to be closed down. The workers had been staging an occupation for around six weeks as we walked past the gates. At the gates they had provided refreshments for the walkers and presented me with cash from a collection they had made among the workers. There was almost £300. This was from people who had earned nothing for weeks and had no idea when their next pay day would be. I found it a really moving gesture and was delighted to read that the following month, Harland and Wolff had been saved.

We flew to Cardiff for the third day's walk which would start at Rodney Parade, home of Newport County and end at the Millennium Stadium. I took some good-natured stick at County as they were the team whose last gasp goal against Notts County had relegated Hartlepool out of the Football League. Midway through the walk, I was with Matt Le Tissier, when a young girl, probably no more than 10 or 11, asked Tiss why we were walking. When he told her, she said her granddad had cancer and gave Matt all the pocket money she had just received.

We caught the train to London where I knew Kammy was waiting to meet me for the final leg. I also knew that we were close to the £1 million target. The moment came as we reached Arsenal's Emirates stadium. Angela Culhane, PCUK's chief executive, announced in a live interview on *Sky Sports News* that we had smashed through the million pound barrier. It was a great feeling for everyone involved – the walkers (who were the real stars – they raised the money), the organisers, the supportive celebrities and me.

We pushed onto Tottenham Hotspur's new ground and the finish line with a spring in our steps – well, almost. As usual I was allowed to go through the finish line first. There clutching my medal was my mate Lloyd Pinder. He hadn't been well enough to walk, but he was determined to be there with me at the end. It was a fitting climax to a wonderful occasion – and I'm sure Irvine Welsh would have found some colourful language in celebration!

12

THE WINNER IS . . .

I have always thought the ultimate accolade in the entertainment business isn't winning awards, but being asked to host them. I've often been envious of Dermot O'Leary at the National Television Awards, Carol Vorderman at the Pride of Britain awards, Stephen Fry or more recently Joanna Lumley at the Baftas or even Phillip Schofield presenting the British Soap awards.

I have never quite reached that level of award ceremony hosting. In fact, I was so far down the pecking order that I accepted the chance to be part of the British Turkey Awards 2014 at the Savoy Hotel in London. I wasn't the main host of this event – that honour fell to Patrick Kielty – but was there to present an award and host the raffle. Now just in case you are wondering, this wasn't an awards ceremony for bad movies or performances, this was just what it said on the tin, or label.

To give you a flavour (pardon the pun) there was an award for the best ready-to-eat product (Nominations: Adlington roasted turkey breast stuffed with ham and wholegrain mustard / Morrisons signature butter-roasted free range turkey breast). Another was for best Christmas convenience product (Nominations: Tesco finest free range bronze turkey crown with pork, bacon and chestnut stuffing / Sainsburys turkey breast and thigh joint with pork, cranberry and apple stuffing topped with cranberry and apricot / Asda turkey breast joint wrapped in bacon / Morrisons Great British stuffed turkey crown). Some tough decisions there.

At least if the awards, eleven of them in all, were less than gripping there was the dinner to look forward to!

— MENU —

Starter
*British turkey bonbon and shredded turkey tian
with split pea hummus*

Main course
*Pomegranate glazed spiced British turkey baton
with saffron potato*

Dessert was the only thing in the whole night that appeared to have no element of turkey in it.

I've used this example to illustrate that if you are not Dermot, Phil, Joanna, Holly or Carol or of that status, not every award ceremony is glitzy. As President of the Television and Radio Industry Club (TRIC) one of my duties was to host their annual bash where I was following some hard acts – Eamonn Holmes, Brian Blessed, Jon Culshaw, Mary Nightingale, Kate Garraway and Sandi Toksvig among them.

I have hosted the League Managers' awards, the Football League awards and the Professional Footballers' Association awards (quite a tough gig to lift the audience as the evening starts with a roll call of members who have died in the preceding 12 months). But in general, you take what you can get.

Football club awards nights should be handled with caution though. You can be booked for these events in January with the club safe in mid-table, only to find a late-season slump has left them relegated. When Ben Shepherd hosted the West Ham United awards the day after they had gone down in 2011, he found himself appealing for calm between the beef main course and the white chocolate truffle dessert as disgruntled fans made their feelings known about the season. The police had to be called – not something that happens often at the Grosvenor House Hotel. I am delighted to say I hosted West Ham's awards in 2019 and this time the beef was followed by the white chocolate truffle, without the threat of a chair landing in your lap. Then again they had not been relegated.

A few years ago, I agreed to fly to Munich to give a speech and host some international awards for the Electrical Industry. I had been told beforehand that the audience would be mainly English speaking and mainly football fans. I was a little late arriving at the venue and needed to go straight on stage. The hostess looking after me asked how long I would speak for before getting to the actual awards. I told her half an hour if it went well, a little less if it wasn't going well. When my name was announced, the lukewarm reaction told me that I might be less than a household name in Munich (perhaps they should have booked Alan McInally!). And the blank looks that greeted my first story told me that most of the 500 people didn't speak English. I leant down towards the hostess. 'Five minutes to the awards, please,' I told her. Apparently the English managing director of the magazine loved *Soccer Saturday* and insisted on having me. After the awards had taken place, I stayed into the early hours telling him the stories I had intended to tell to the guests. Hopefully, he felt he hadn't completely wasted his company's money.

Another event which I suspected wasn't going to be a rip-roaring success was closer to home. I had been booked to speak at the end of a finance conference at a swish hotel in London's Park Lane. This was the final event after two days of meetings and lectures and as soon as I had finished, everyone could go. As I stood up to speak, a woman's voice from the centre of the room said loudly, 'Oh my god, not another middle-aged white man in a suit talking about football.' I didn't delay the audience too much, reckoning brevity was the order of the day. It was only later that I found out that Matt Le Tissier had done the job the previous year. And Paul Merson the year before.

Sometimes you get a sense of foreboding even before the event. I was asked to host a night in a marquee in the Channel Islands at which the highlight would be *A Question of Sport* between three ex-rugby union play-ers and three ex-professional footballers including, I recall, Neil 'Razor' Ruddock. The organisers sent me a list of questions beforehand, 20 of them as they didn't want this section of the night to run too long. Every single question was based on rugby union! I asked the organisers to have a rethink or else I would provide the questions myself. I didn't think Razor and his team-mates would be too pleased otherwise. The night was chaotic. My introduction to the evening's events was performed to a backdrop of a live World Cup game on two giant screens complete with low level commentary.

It is fair to say I did not have the crowd in the palm of my hand. Later, I conducted an auction for an autographed football shirt, only to find when it was brought on stage it had more than a passing resemblance to a cricket shirt autographed by Michael Vaughan. When the comedian came on, a couple of his gags were aimed at the rugby boys. One slipped out to the back of the marquee, quietly crawled under the canvas onto the stage and rugby tackled the unsuspecting comedian, sending him flying off the stage, down a three-foot drop and hitting the floor hard. That was the end of the comedy and pretty much the end of the night.

Things can get out of hand pretty quickly. I remember being asked to speak at an awards ceremony in Glasgow and being shocked when the organisers told me I would be on stage at 8 pm. I explained that I usually liked people to have had a drink or two before I spoke. 'Och, they will have,' I was assured. And they had! Before I spoke some impromptu dancing had left an elderly Scot flat out on his back in the middle of the room, kilt hoisted above his waist. Of course, he was wearing nothing beneath it. It was enough to put me off my meal of meat and two veg.

On an earlier visit to Glasgow, I had been warned the 600-strong audience could be a tough crowd. The previous year's host – who announced himself as 'the best after-dinner speaker in England' – had been removed from stage after less than five minutes. He was told he might be the best in England, but he would not be speaking in Scotland again for a very long time. No pressure on me, then.

Every awards ceremony, no matter how strange it seems to us, should be treated with respect, as to those nominated and especially the winners, it can be the biggest day of the year. The Industrial Agents' Society awards, for example, is basically assessing the merits of one empty warehouse compared with another. I did my best, but one of the judges who was sitting next to me at lunch told me confidentially this was his first and last year. 'How can you judge one bloody empty space with another empty space?' he said.

I was guest speaker in a freezing cold warehouse – not an award winner, I don't think – at a ceremony in Newcastle for a gas company. Workers had been bussed in from all over the north of England including a group of hefty, well-muscled road diggers, who were less than impressed to be offered non-alcoholic mocktails on their arrival. This was a booze-free event. It was the first time the road diggers had been invited to this particular bash and they left hoping it was the last. Lunch was a fish finger sized piece of cod with half a dozen chips followed by their one-tenth share of a box of Celebrations, washed down by limitless Coca-Cola, orange juice or water. The entertainment was a drumming group whose aim was to teach people to play in 20 minutes. They had brought dozens of spare drums and pieces of percussion with them – enough for around half the guests. That left the other half, including the road diggers, cold, hungry, thirsty and unable to hear a word each other said, deafened by the cacophony of noise from a hundred trainee drummers. They couldn't even go outside for a fag as temperatures were Arctic! The truth is that when I got up to speak, I could hardly fail to go down well, as everything that had gone before was so awful. As the road diggers got back into the bus to head home, the organiser asked me if I would be interested in hosting next year's event.

'I'll just have to check my diary,' I said.

Sometimes though things turn out unexpectedly well, even when some of the audience is not really there to see you. I got a last-minute offer of a well-paid job at the Scottish football club, Cove Rangers. It was so last minute that someone had obviously pulled out and they had – Harry Redknapp. I was more than a bit apprehensive about stepping into the shoes of the 'King of the Jungle', especially when people had paid to see him, not me. I needn't have worried. 'I know some of you are disappointed that I am here instead of Harry. It's not you,' I said, pointing at a nearby table.

'And it's not you,' pointing at a second. And turning to a third, 'but it might be you!' It ended up being one of the best events I have been involved in.

But it was still a long way from the Baftas!

13

FALLING OUT

DAVE JONES

Stelling . . . the letter began. Not promising. Worse still, the correspondence was on the preferred paper of those who write abuse, lined and ripped from a wirebound notepad. I have toned down the content for those who are easily offended (and indeed for those not easily offended) and added punctuation so that the message is clearer.

> You c*** getting Dave Jones the sack. You arrogant c***. Happy now? How would you like the sack from Sky you t***? Hope your s*** Hartlepool goes down, you prik. You are a prik, a***hole who knows f*** all. Grow up Stelling, you prik. Rot with Hartlepool prik.
>
> Mr C Young
> Cry baby a***hole prik

I realise a lot of the words are asterisked, but I hope you get the general feeling. His outburst came after I had called for the Hartlepool manager Dave Jones to quit or be sacked in 2017 after we had dropped into the League Two relegation places following a home defeat by Barnet. Jones had won just three of his 17 games in charge and my outburst had been born out of desperation.

Mr C Young was not alone in his defence of Jones. Two weeks later after the club had been relegated to the National League, I received another letter on lined paper and ripped from a wirebound notepad, this time written in block capitals.

STELLING,
    JUST TO SAY I AM THRILLED HARTLEPOOL HAVE GONE DOWN YOU T***. THAT'S ONE FOR DAVE JONES YOU T***. UP YOURS STELLING. LAUGH THAT OFF HA HA PRIK.
    YOURS TRULY
    T ROBSON

You may get the impression that these letters were perhaps the work of the same person, but I could not possibly comment.

I am fortunate that in over four decades of broadcasting I have had very few fallouts although anyone who sits near me will know that sometimes when I go to a game I find it hard to keep myself in check. When Gillingham's Max Ehmer ran half the length of the pitch to celebrate provocatively in front of Hartlepool fans after they scored a late FA Cup winner, I could not resist giving him a verbal volley as he left the field. I apologised to the chairman and chief exec first and then yelled, 'Ehmer, Ehmer!' Max looked up. 'That's how we will celebrate when your lot get relegated, pal.' Pathetic, but I had to get it off my chest. The truth is, if he had been playing for us we would have won! But some fall-outs are on a wholly different level.

When Dave Jones was appointed Hartlepool manager, I was fully behind the decision. It would be his first managerial role for four years but his CV could not have been better for a club clinging to the Football League status it had held for 96 years and I felt Chairman Gary Coxall had made a good decision. In February, I had gone for a drink with Jones in his office after a 4–0 win over Crewe. Even then I was a little concerned when he told me he had hammered young full-back Kenton Richardson for crossing the halfway line to create the third goal.

The win was a false dawn. Results got worse, not better. I spoke with the chairman on a regular basis but never attempted to influence team selection. Obviously with working on Saturdays, I didn't see them enough to know who was playing well and who wasn't. A string of defeats meant that the team travelled to Leyton Orient on Easter Monday in desperate need of a win. The East London club was in turmoil looking sure to be relegated. Their players hadn't been paid for weeks and the crowd was protesting against the owner. They played a virtual youth team but still beat us. Our starting line-up that day included Padraig Amond, who went on to score goals against Man City, Spurs and Leicester during two seasons in which he top scored at Newport; Liam Donnelly who was top scorer for Motherwell in the SPL before corona-virus intervened; Nathan Thomas who two months later would be signed by Sheffield United; Brad Walker who is now with League One Shrewsbury. And yet the manager could not get a performance out of them to beat a bunch of kids. Defeat against Barnet on the Saturday almost sealed our fate. I could not hold back.

'This is not personal Dave, but Dave Jones, for god's sake, for the good of the club walk now, go now, this is not your level of football. Chairman Gary Coxall, if he won't walk, sack him. If it means me resigning as club President I will do so happily. Do it now. Do it today'.

It was of course unprofessional. But I love that football club. It had been my life for decades, whereas for Dave it was just another club after Stockport, Southampton, Wolves, Cardiff and Sheffield Wednesday.

Two days later he was sacked. Jones complained to the LMA, the League Managers' Association. I was hauled over the coals by Sky and rang Richard Bevan, chief executive of the LMA, to explain the reasons for my outburst. I heard nothing more from them.

To understand this was no vendetta from me, read what Nick Loughlin, a respected sportswriter had to say about the Jones regime in the *Northern Echo* after his dismissal.

'Jones' whole reign was a bewildering one . . . He frustrated club staff with his constant demands. He was testing them, seeing how far he could push them, but they felt ridiculed by him as he constantly belittled the club from within. It is fair to say the club was a happier place yesterday as downtrodden staff returned to work with smiles on their faces.'

Our paths have not crossed since, which is just as well judging by his reaction when asked about me by the *Wolf Whistle* podcast in March 2020.

'He is a prat. Everybody can have a say but I was in a position where I had gone and tried to help the club. It is not as if the club was top of the league every year. Every year they struggled to stay in the league and their time was coming to go out. I went in and tried to change it and what was the mistake? We probably tried to change it too quickly at the end of the day.

When people have built up empires within football clubs, they don't want to let it go and those empires needed to be broken as I did when I went to Cardiff and Southampton. You have got to embrace change and they didn't want change.

'I used to get on okay with him but it was cheap journalism and it is not as if he is a football guru. I heard he was phoning the chairman up and asking why I wasn't playing this player and I know a lot of people had a go at him about it, but I have had worse in my life. To me he is a nobody. He tried to use his fame. I would probably knock him out if I saw him. If he was on fire, I wouldn't waste any water, put it that way.'

THE LMA

For years I hosted the League Managers' Association annual awards dinner. It was a great event with many of the game's top managers there. Sir Alex Ferguson for example would always attend. He would usually be the first one in the dining area to make sure he was sitting next to someone he liked – Walter Smith would be first choice – rather than a sponsor. But a discussion on *Soccer Saturday* led to me falling out of favour with the LMA.

In 2006, Les Reed had been a surprise choice to replace Ian Dowie, who had been sacked as manager by Charlton. Les had worked for the FA in a variety of roles, including technical director. He had written *The Official FA Guide to Basic Team Coaching*. But he had never managed. It didn't go well. Charlton had lost 5–1 at Tottenham, 3–0 at home to Liverpool and their solitary win was with an added-time goal at home to Blackburn. The Charlton fans who had loved him when he was Alan Curbishley's assistant during their promotion to the Premier League season were not so sure now. Les was old school too, hard to get a smile out of and a soft target for criticism, to be honest. When we were sent a piece of coaching advice written by him on the importance of looking smart and having socks pulled up when coming out of the dressing room, the *Soccer Saturday* panel went to town.

The LMA wrote a letter of complaint, but Head of Sport Vic Wakeling decided that it had been a balanced discussion as I had at times attempted to put a positive spin on events. Charlton lost 2–0 at Middlesbrough on 23 December and the following day, Christmas Eve, they sacked Les Reed. The LMA never asked me to host an event again and I have never been invited to their awards night since.

I have often wondered if we were a little harsh on Les

that day but he has had the last laugh by going on to help produce some wonderful young players at Southampton and eventually rejoining the England set-up.

SAM ALLARDYCE

I had known and respected Sam for many years before our fallout in 2006. I'd been at plenty of Bolton matches and he had been on our panel once or twice. I had seen at first hand the spirit he engendered in the squad when I bumped into them at a Hampshire health resort celebrating a big win at Portsmouth. Everyone from the youngest kids to the most senior pro joined in the party.

And it was Portsmouth against Bolton again when the incident that came nearest to costing me my job happened.

Sam had been one of the subjects of a *Panorama* investigation on BBC TV alleging he had been involved in illegal dealings, allegations which he has always denied. I had no reason to disbelieve Sam, but the following week when I was hosting from Fratton Park, I took the chance to ask him in the live interview after the game. I honestly believed this was just a chance for Sam to further emphasise there was nothing in the allegations.

I asked Sam if he had ever been offered a bung – not taken one.

'You are out of order asking me that,' said Sam. The scanner, the outside broadcasting control truck housing the director, producer and assistant producers had fallen completely silent until I heard a solitary voice say, 'Why the fuck did he ask him that?'

Sam finished the interview and we somehow got off air. I was warned not to go near the tunnel area as the then Bolton chairman Phil Gartside wanted my blood. I sneaked out of Fratton Park by a back door. In an effort to pre-empt the approaching storm, I rang Vic Wakeling. It was too late. No hello Jeff, how are you Jeff. 'What the fuck have you done? Phil Gartside has just been on the phone tearing my head off.' Bolton were threatening to boycott Sky. BBC 5 Live called to ask if I wanted to go on their hour-long phone-in the following morning with Victoria Derbyshire. Surprisingly I did not. The only saving grace for me was that most of the national press supported me the following day, praising me for asking the question that everyone wanted to hear answered. I was at pains to point out to anyone who would listen that I only asked if he had ever been offered a bung, not taken one – a huge difference.

Sky made me sweat. I was told that Vic and Andy Melvin, his combative No 2, wanted to see me but not for two weeks. In the meantime, I had to carry on not knowing whether I would have a job in a fortnight's time. When the meeting came I told Vic that I thought the question was journalistically the correct one to ask, but said I was sorry for the trouble it had caused. I repeated this two or three times, but they persisted in asking the same question until I blurted out. 'I have said I am sorry Vic, I can't do any more than that, if you are going to sack me just do it and get it over with!' After a brief pause, Vic simply said, 'Get out of my sight.' The meeting was over.

It took a long time to build bridges with Sam. I wanted to speak to him personally, but he was bruised. Phil Brown and Peter Reid spoke to him on my behalf more than once. Eventually we arranged to talk on the phone where I tried to explain that I had only wanted to give him an opportunity to shoot down the *Panorama* allegations. A couple of years went by before we bumped into each other and had a drink together. Later he would appear on the *Soccer Saturday* panel. I am not sure I will ever be on his Christmas card list, but these days we are fine again.

I survived in a job, but the producer Steve Tudgay left the company at the end of that season and, in my heart, I suspect it was down to the Fratton Park incident, which was harsh as he had no advance knowledge of me asking the question.

Would I ask the same question again now? I honestly don't know the answer to that.

SIR ALEX FERGUSON

'**Manchester United boss Sir Alex Ferguson forgets his manners at Football Writers' do!**' was the *Daily Mail* headline.

It was nothing more than a storm in a teacup. I am fortunate enough never to have had the legendary hair dryer treatment from Sir Alex. In truth, our paths rarely crossed apart from at LMA functions. The Man United boss had agreed to a live interview on *Soccer Saturday* on one occasion and despite a threatening water sprinkler, it went well. Or it did until I asked a question he didn't much like.

'You normally ask sensible questions, Jeff,' said Sir Alex. 'So why have you asked such a stupid one now?'

'Charlie Nicholas told me to ask it, Sir Alex,' I blurted, sounding like a schoolboy who had been found smoking behind the bike sheds but trying to shift the blame elsewhere.

The Football Writers' 'do' in question was to honour Wayne Rooney as Player of the Year. There have been some wonderfully eloquent winners in the past few years, Frank Lampard, Steven Gerrard and Thierry Henry among them, and the Football Writers' Association wanted to make Wayne more comfortable when it came to making his acceptance speech. They employed me to interview him to hopefully relax and bring the best out of him.

Unfortunately, his agent wanted to turn this into the most embarrassing interview in the history of the FWA. He presented me with a list of questions which must have come straight from the pages of *Shoot!* 'Apart from Man United which is your favourite team?' 'Who is your toughest opponent?' 'Who is your favourite band?' 'What was your favourite film?' I caught Wayne before the event started and told him I could not ask those questions or we would both be laughing stocks. I told him to trust me and I wouldn't embarrass him. As it happens he was superb: honest, eloquent and funny.

I remember asking him why he felt he had scored so many headed goals that season. He said that in previous seasons, Cristiano Ronaldo would beat his man and he would make his run, only for Ronaldo to try and beat his man again and again. After making his run time and again without the ball being delivered by the Portuguese star, Wayne would stop making them. Ronaldo had now left the club to join Real Madrid.

'This season I make the run, Antonio Valencia crosses first time and I score!' said Wayne.

I was aware of Sir Alex making a few grumbling noises, almost under his breath but within earshot. But I think it was when I asked who was the scariest manager Wayne had played under, Fergie or Fabio Capello, that he very audibly came out with, 'Oh for god's sake, Jeff.' Clearly Wayne heard it too and his answers became much more clipped than before. It didn't matter as the interview was almost over and Wayne had shone. Afterwards, I pointed out to Sir Alex I had been employed by the FWA, not him, and that the interview length was pre-agreed. Later the likes of Peter Reid and David Moyes assured him that it had gone well and his star striker had only enhanced his reputation.

But the hairdryer? I've felt hotter at Toni and Guy.

SCUNTHORPE CHAIRMAN PETER SWANN

In October 2014 Scunthorpe United sacked their manager Russ Wilcox. To say it was harsh was an understatement and I made that clear in a Sky Sports online comment piece.

'Obviously, I am an outsider and I don't see Scun-thorpe play, while people will point to the fact that since January he has won nine out of 32 games. But this was the man who had a record breaking 28-game unbeaten run when he took over, got them promotion, played for them for six years, was assistant manager, caretaker manager and manager. What did that buy him? Eleven games in a higher division. Chairman Peter Swann came out and said, "Now was the right time. We respect Russ a huge amount for what he did." No, you didn't. You would not have sacked him if you had respected him a huge amount.'

Unsurprisingly, the chairman was not best pleased and made his feelings plain to Sky Sports. I challenged him to come onto the show live the following week to explain the sacking. Knowing Peter now, I should not have been surprised that he took up the challenge. The following Saturday there was a bruising encounter as Peter defended himself fiercely, telling me just what he thought of my analysis of his decision and just what he thought of me. At the end, I thought it magnanimous to say that it had been a hard-fought draw.

'You must be joking,' said Swann. 'I won that hands down!'

The great thing was that out of our argument came a friendship. Peter supported my marathon walks by taking part in them with his wife. And when Prostate Cancer UK auctioned off a day in the *Soccer Saturday* studios at a fund-raising event, the successful bidder was none other than the Scunthorpe chairman himself, Peter Swann.

THOMMO

Fallouts with Phil Thompson? Every week.

THE VIDIPRINTER

Soccer Saturday could – and will – survive without me. It could survive without Matt Le Tissier, Paul Merson, Phil Thompson and Charlie Nicholas. The only irreplaceable element of the show is the vidiprinter.

Every week my biggest nightmare is if the vidiprinter breaks down. Which is exactly what happened on the opening day of the 2013 Football League season. The first day of any new campaign is tough for me as many players have switched clubs and there's often a big intake of new tongue-twisting names from abroad.

Like the *Titanic* heading towards the iceberg, we had sailed serenely along for 40 minutes when, with no warning, scores stopped coming through. I could hear the panic in the gallery as we tried to find out what the problem was. Time ticked by with no resolution. Half-time came and went. Deep into the second half I could hold back no longer. Going into a commercial break, I went into full John Cleese mode.

'Listen here. I am warning you. If you don't get your act together, I am going to thrash you!' I yelled at the still inactive vidiprinter. Of course, it made no difference. During the break I borrowed a hammer from a technician and when we came back live I gave my best impression of smashing the thing to pieces.

An hour and half later, the problem was resolved. But by then all the games were finished, as was my relationship with the company who were providing the vidiprinter service.

THOMAS CRAIG

The Sheffield Wednesday-supporting *Coronation Street* star was interviewed alongside me on *Soccer AM* before the 2005 play-off final against Hartlepool. Less than two months earlier, he had been killed off in the long-running TV soap by his daughter Katy, who hit him over the head with a wrench. When he told Tim Lovejoy that

Sheffield Wednesday would deserve to win because they are a 'big club', I raised an eyebrow. But when he added it was just a lovely day out for the supporters of Hartlepool, I told him, 'Clearly Katy did the right thing by hitting you over the head with that wrench!'

FOOTBALL365

I didn't have a fallout with the website Football365 but they certainly seemed to have had a fallout with *Soccer Saturday* in 2017. Of course, individuals or programmes should always expect to take the rough with the smooth and this site had always been very positive about both me and the show. But in April of that year they hammered us.

'The people behind *Soccer Saturday* deliberately employ some pundits who are less than intelligent. They see it as reflecting part of the audience back to themselves. The uneducated, intellectually undernourished punter loves Merse because he talks like them and is endearingly funny. They love that he can't say foreign names because they can't either. They don't see a stupid bloke with limited vocabulary. They see a fun bloke who got rich playing football and is still one of them. If you put a lot of clever people on *Soccer Saturday* a lot would turn off. They want simple ideas, presented by simple people and that's what they get. And that's why it has been successful for so long.'

Clearly Football365 also employed some people who are less than intelligent. In all the years I have presented the show, that is the single most stupid article I have ever read.

14

TIME FOR A BREAK

From time to time, for reasons best known to themselves, companies choose to employ one or all of the *Soccer Saturday* team for commercials. Sometimes these are very straightforward. Buxton Water employed me to say a four-word voice-over at the end of an advert. They booked a recording studio for two hours. Now, there are only so many variations of tone, emphasis, gravitas and pace that you can do when delivering four words. Ten minutes into the session we had been through every possible alternative. The producer was happy and I was even happier having finished so quickly, though I wasn't sure that my contribution would have made the same impact as that of Maria Sharapova who was advertising rival brand Evian. Twelve months on though and Buxton rang my agent to say they wanted to renew the deal for a further year. This time they didn't need me to do anything new. They were the best paid four words I have ever said.

I have been paid for delivering fewer words though. I recorded an advert in south London for the brewers Carlsberg, with the title 'If Carlsberg Did Kickabouts' with the legendary ex Manchester United and Denmark goalkeeper Peter Schmeichel. My role consisted of opening a caravan door and saying, 'Oh my word' as players in the kickabout produced world-class footballing feats, inspired of course by a pint of frothing golden lager. I must have opened that caravan door 30 times before the director was happy, but I could hardly complain. Still I had it tough compared to Schmeichel, who earned his fee without saying a single word. All he had to do was catch a football – something I think he has done once or twice in the past.

But other times can be much more complicated, especially when either Kammy or Merse is involved.

I went to Yorkshire to record a commercial for Papa John's Pizza. It was a short-notice job, but as you would expect good dough! I learned my lines the night before the shoot. Kammy hadn't worried about such a trifling thing. Instead he loaded his section of the script onto the autocue app on his mobile phone, which he could then attach under the camera so he could simply read his lines. Unfortunately, the camera was some distance away and regular viewers to *Soccer Saturday* will know Kammy finds it hard to see things at the best of times. He simply could not read the lines. That was his problem. Mine was that every time we started a take, I would be required to take a bite from a pristine Pepperoni, Sausage & Six Cheese pizza. When Kammy fluffed his lines, a new pizza would be provided for me to bite into. After five or six takes, the crew was starting to find the whole thing funny, which made it even harder for him to get it right. After 10, we needed a new batch of pizzas. After 15, my stomach was beginning to rebel. After 20, I knew I would never eat a pizza again.

Kammy was involved again when *Soccer Saturday* sponsors Gillette wanted a series of new break-bumpers filmed at an incredibly posh house in Ham, southwest London. Bumpers are the short pieces going into and out of advertising breaks. Unsurprisingly, it involved us shaving. The snag was that we had to shave without the benefit of a mirror as the camera would have been seen in the reflection. Effectively we were shaving blindfold. Kammy was first and this time he was perfect and precise, his pencil thin moustache untouched, the rest of his face bristle free. I survived too without too much trouble. Then it was the turn of Merse. Within moments, his face was streaming with blood. Never has a director's call of 'Cut!' been more apt. Try as they may, neither

Merse, make-up nor the medic could stem the flow. The shoot was abandoned. Only Kammy and I would appear on the new Gillette break-bumpers.

Merse had a speaking role in Sky Sports' 'Take Your Seat' campaign promo a couple of seasons ago. This was a big budget opener to a new football season with a bigger cast than *Ben Hur*. Paul, Charlie, Phil and Matt had to push me down a south London street as I reclined on a two-seater sofa. Dozens of extras carrying settees, chairs, stools and cushions ran alongside. A breathless Merse had to gasp out, 'Are you comfy there, Jeff?' as everyone – except me – ran. But Merse decided to ad lib, 'Are you comfortable enough, Jeff?' he said. 'Hope you are comfortable on the sofa, Jeff,' and came out with every other possible combination of words. Every time he got it wrong, the whole cast would have to drag sofas, chairs, stools and cushions back to the top of the street and start again. It was an exhausting shoot. Except for me.

Martin Tyler, the 'Voice' as he is known throughout football, was involved in the same shoot though not on the same day as us. Apparently the director, sitting in his director's chair with 'Director' written on the back in case we were unaware of his importance, was not a football lover. He didn't know any of us. But he was unhappy at the way Martin delivered his lines and told him so. I have no way of knowing if this is true, except that the director was still breathing when we turned up the following day. Martin would not have been amused by the criticism, though I have to confess we were!

Merse and I were also together for a *Sky Sports Fantasy Football* advert in 2013 along with Fenners, John Fendley of *Soccer AM* fame. All three of us were overshadowed by Big Mouth Billy Bass, a speaking fish who had been a craze in the late 1990s. The only one with a speaking part was the fish!

Sky Broadband ran a campaign featuring Bruce Willis and then came up with the idea of recreating it using me – I am guessing I was cheaper. It had exactly the same opening shot, except that instead of Willis stepping out of a lift in his dressing gown, I did. They used exactly the same actors and set, even the same dressing gown. Just like Willis, I got the girl in the end with the most unlikely chat-up line ever.

'Come on, let me show you round Hartlepool,' I said as she mouthed silently, 'Where's Hartlepool?' It is my favourite ad of those I have been involved in.

I worked with Carlsberg for a number of years, often on live events. They were terrific to work with but there was one small drawback. I was obliged to wear a specially made suit, shirt and tie all made in Carlsberg green at every event. I got some looks when I stopped for petrol or a snack on the way to the venues. In 2014,

I did a World Cup television commercial for them with Ian Wright and Paddy McGuinness. The idea was that we would transform the pub viewing experience for football fans. Paddy was the landlord of 'The Eternal Optimist' serving ice-cold Carlsberg on a sushi-style conveyor belt to thirsty fans. As usual dressed in my green suit, I pressed a magic beer mat and a giant state of the art TV rose out of the floor of the pub to replace the tiny tired set that fans were gathered round. Ian had a direct link to the referee of a crucial England game and persuaded him to change his mind over awarding a penalty. It was a lot of fun working with Paddy and Ian as you can imagine. But it was also very technical and took an eternity, even though the ad would only run for 60 seconds. Late on the third day of filming, we were asked to do one final shot 'just one more time'. We must have already done it 20 or 30 times. Paddy and I were thinking the same thing, but it was Ian who exploded. 'No, not just one more time, no more times, you have got it, we are done, finished.' The shot never appeared in the advert and I have never loved Wrighty more for speaking out.

I am not sure if Carlsberg is probably the best beer in the world or not, but they are certainly right up there when it comes to advertising. Four years earlier I had been in another pre-World Cup commercial featuring the most ridiculously stellar cast. In 90 seconds there were appearances from Stuart Pearce, Jack Charlton, Sir Trevor Brooking, Phil 'The Power' Taylor, Sir Ranulph Fiennes, Sir Ian Botham, Sir Steve Redgrave, Sir Clive Woodward, Nigel Benn, Ellen MacArthur, Dame Kelly Holmes, Carl Fogarty, Kasabian and me! How did I get in among that company? It was filmed at The Den in Millwall with my role to leap in front of the England team as they came out of the tunnel, naked from the waist up, a huge Cross of St George painted across my chest, and give a banshee wail. Even the headmaster at my sons' rather posh school said it was 'an interesting look'. It was a great experience but I was in a rush to get away at the end of the shoot. Rather than remove the deep red paint from my chest, one of the make-up artists filled an empty Evian water bottle to the brim with white spirit so I could clean myself up when I got home. Goodness knows what my fellow passengers on the 17.05 to Winchester made of what must have looked like a thick slash of blood at the top of my chest, visible at the open-neck of my shirt. The most worrying thing though was that in the scramble to get off the train, I accidentally left the Evian bottle full of white spirit on the table where I had been sitting. I could only hope and pray that no-one suddenly felt thirsty before the train reached its final destination.

I have often thought if Carlsberg did football shows, would any of them resemble *Soccer Saturday* a little?

15

MAN OF LETTERS

It was late in 2018 when I received a letter that truly was unique.

> Dear Jeff, my husband and I are big fans of yours.
> We really miss Alphabetical so much (We love Soccer Saturday too). Can you tell me when it is coming back please?
> Best wishes
> Shirley Johnson

The letter was unique because after two series and 30 episodes, it was the only letter I had ever received asking about the show *Alphabetical*. Unfortunately, I had to tell Shirley that it would not be coming back at all (or not in the foreseeable future, as ITV put it).

Alphabetical was based on a TV show in Spain, *Pasapalabra*, that has run for more than two decades.

We managed two series. In Spain, they gave away jackpot prizes in their millions. We didn't have a single winner. After the first series, the website UKGameShows.com voted it the worst new game show of 2016. They did admit though, that done slightly differently, the show could have figured on the site's Hall of Fame instead of the Hall of Shame. One of the things they would have done slightly differently I think, was to pick someone other than me to host it!

I had done three years on *Countdown* with Rachel Riley and Susie Dent and loved it. We tried to give the classic old show a slightly more contemporary feel by introducing different guests like Tim Vine, Jon Culshaw and Dave Spikey. I still remember tears rolling down my face as Dave told his story of getting a pair of knitted swimming trunks as a gift for his birthday. They were less than flattering in a certain department for a teenage boy, so a friend advised him to put a carrot down them. Dave did, only to find the girls were repelled rather than impressed. His friend told him the carrot should have gone down the front of the trunks, not the back!

We introduced sportsmen too. Cricketer David Lloyd and *Soccer Saturday's* Matt Le Tissier were regular guests in 'Dictionary Corner'. I even managed to persuade Premier League footballer Clarke Carlisle of Burnley to be a contestant. He was a revelation with four straight wins.

To this day I am certain he could have gone on to win more, but he suddenly lost his form. Perhaps the fact that he would have to miss training for a second day to continue on the show the following day was a conundrum for him. He certainly didn't fit the stereotype that footballers are thick. Matt would also be a contestant, though by that time Nick Hewer was in the chair. Tiss also notched a string of wins.

Even though *Countdown* was pressurised, it had quite a laid-back feel. Effectively with Rachel and Susie alongside me, there were three presenters, so there was always a little breathing space.

Helter-skelter, 100 miles an hour *Alphabetical* though was a very different beast.

I had been asked to do two pilot shows in two days by ITV. One was a television version of Scrabble, which has yet to see the light of day. The other was *Alphabetical*. The idea of the show was that contestants would accrue time in the first part of the show to add to the 100 seconds they were given to answer 26 questions, each answer beginning with one specific letter of the alphabet. If a contestant didn't know the right answer they bewilderingly had to say 'alphabetical' rather than 'pass'. It had one basic problem – it was impossible to win. The jackpot rose, game after game, and a solitary winner would have made newspaper headlines and probably guaranteed the future of the show. But to be honest it never looked like being won. The questions were too long. Many people thought I read them too slowly, but it was tough to go any quicker without stumbling or mispronouncing names. Forget the answers, try reading out 26 questions and see how long it takes!

In Spain, viewers were more patient than in the UK. David Garcia, a professional gamer, appeared on their version 100 times between March and October 2016. Thirteen times he came within one correct answer of winning. But every time he failed, the jackpot increased. When he finally did get all 26 questions right, his prize was 1.8 million Euros. That wasn't even the record. Eduardo Benito from Madrid took home 2.2 million Euros.

One contributor to UKGameShows.com gave his appraisal of our effort. 'You cannot have a show where the end game is impossible to win. Why would anyone watch once they realise that? Dull presentation, terrible hosting and quite frankly we don't need any more word/letter games in my lifetime.'

At the end of the second series another wrote: 'So after all this nobody wins. What a waste!'

Despite that, my understanding is that *Tenable* with Warwick Davis got the nod to continue ahead of *Alphabetical* by the finest of margins.

I felt for Adam Adler who had been the man behind

the show, as he had invested years of his life into it. It did produce though one of the great quizzing answers during its run. Asked to name a game or sport that you might see taking place in a pub, our contestant replied 'Dog Fighting!' Now I have been in some tough pubs in my time . . .

I was offered a chance to present an ITV game show called *Freeze Out*, a curling-based quiz, but could not because of a diary clash. Mark Durden-Smith, an old friend of mine, got the hosting role. The *Guardian* described it as 'the game show that is so bad it makes you question the whole concept of game shows'. UKGameShows.com voted it the worst game show of 2015. My hosting track record could have looked pretty ugly if I had done that one too.

It is incredibly difficult for a game show to establish itself against hugely successful rivals like *Pointless*, *The Chase* and *Who Wants To Be A Millionaire* and the networks are littered with flops. Would I do another game show if I was asked? Pass – or should I say, 'Alphabetical!'

One thing about being a C-list celebrity is you do get asked on a lot of shows. Most of them I have turned down on the basis of not wanting to make an idiot of myself. Many years ago, I did beat Steve Ryder to win a sports presenters' version of *The Weakest Link* but that was a bit of a fluke – I got easy questions in the final, he got impossible ones. More recently I was asked onto *Celebrity Mastermind* and told the questions would be dumbed down and I could pick Hartlepool United FC as my specialist subject. But it would hardly do my credibility much good if I did as athlete Kadeena Cox did a few years ago when she scored three points on her specialist subject Arsenal FC and none at all on general knowledge. I wasn't even sure I would get any more. I declined – a rare sensible decision.

I was asked to be part of a celebrity team on *Pointless* – a show in which the jackpot is almost as tough to win as *Alphabetical*. My team-mate would be Kammy, whose track record in quiz shows is less than impressive. Thankfully, I was out of the country. He was paired with Melinda Messenger, a result for him. They were first out. A result for me!

I have relented a bit lately though and my team of Anita Rani, Hannah Cockcroft, A J Pritchard and Tom Rosenthal actually did really well in *The Crystal Maze*, but I blew a seemingly unassailable lead against Charlotte Hawkins and Andy Whyment in *Catchphrase* and was first out in *Tipping Point: Lucky Stars*. I was consoled though by Ben Shepherd who told me I had done far better than Kammy, who in response to the question 'What grows in paddy fields?' answered 'Potatoes'. I still feel game shows are not my forte.

My judgement may not be too strong either. On an edition of *The X Factor* spin-off show, *The Xtra Factor*, I told Rylan Clark-Neal that his best chance of a future in show business was on kids' TV! After seeing him on *Strictly Come Dancing: It Takes Two*, *The One Show*, *Ready Steady Cook*, *Supermarket Sweep* and a thousand other things, perhaps I was a bit hasty.

I think the chances of me appearing on anything requiring physical prowess are fading by the day. I am in awe of those like Helen Skelton, Nikki Sanderson and Brendan Cole on shows like *Celebrity SAS: Who Dares Wins* as they abseil down sheer cliff faces and are submerged in freezing seas. Not for me, though I do love the celebrity version of *Hunted* and was hugely jealous when my Sky colleague Kay Burley got invited to take part a couple of series ago.

One other show I would love to take part in – like many other people – is *I'm a Celebrity . . . Get Me Out of Here!* I am a bit afraid of heights, not a very good swimmer, a picky eater and not fond of snakes, so I would be ideal for the public to torture in Bushtucker trials. In 2019, I got an interview which I felt went pretty well. I knew I was in the final 40 or so (because they only interview 40 or so!). But when I heard the rumours that Ian Wright was on the shortlist, I feared the worst. The show wasn't going to have two people from the football world, albeit at opposite ends of the spectrum, on the same series. Still, they do like to have at least one contestant from the older generation – Stanley Johnson was 77 – so perhaps time is still on my side!

16

THE ROAD SHOW

On 26 January 2016 I received an e-mail from my solicitor.

> **Good Afternoon. I am the bearer of very good news.
> They are offering a drop hands settlement with no
> obligation to do any more shows. There you have it,
> a complete capitulation.**

I did not regard it as any sort of capitulation in truth, but it was the end of a four-year legal nightmare that cost me personally £250,000 and left me totally disillusioned with English law.

It had all started towards the end of 2011, when the popular comedian Mike Osman approached the team through his friend Matt Le Tissier. He wanted to stage a *Soccer Saturday Live* tour taking in some of England's biggest cities. As most of the boys already did their own after-dinner shows and had some great tales to tell, it seemed a no-brainer. We would perform in a one-off show at the Mayflower Theatre in Southampton and if it went well, would draw up plans to take it nationwide. In fact rather than being a no-brainer, it turned out to be a brainless decision from all of us.

The first show itself was incredibly low-tech. Just Mike Osman with the warm-up, then myself hosting a Q&A session on stage with Tiss, Merse, Charlie and Thommo with the addition of a few props and some slides. The Mayflower was packed to almost its 2,300 capacity and the show was a huge success. We went to a local restaurant afterwards and agreed to try and put together a five-city tour. I didn't pick up the bill, but it was the most expensive meal of my life.

After a number of meetings, it was decided the venues would be Bournemouth, London, Birmingham, Liverpool and Newcastle. Tickets would be sold through agency Live Nation. The venues would take some filling – among them the Metro Arena, the Liverpool Echo Arena, the Birmingham National Indoor Arena and Wembley Arena, all of them enormous.

The first night was in March at the Bournemouth International Centre, a huge venue, but an encouragingly big crowd had turned up. Kammy was involved this time, not on the panel but singing and as a roving reporter. Harry Redknapp was our special guest. Even before becoming 'King of the Jungle', Harry could fill pretty much any venue. We had recruited top Sky producer Ian Condron, then working on *Soccer Saturday* and a former Premier League producer, to ensure that things went smoothly. There was a meet and greet beforehand, snazzy, high-quality colour programmes on sale and the show was much more high-tech this time with proper sound systems and video.

It was an unqualified success in the eyes of everyone who had been there. Lorelei Reddin wrote an article in the *Bournemouth Echo* that was so complimentary about the evening, we should have asked her to write our advertising copy: 'an evening of hilarious and insightful football anecdotes'; 'the perfect night out for football fans'; 'wonderful raconteurs'; 'tremendous fun, great entertainment and I enjoyed it almost as much as watching the Saints at the moment'.

Not the sort of review you might expect from a show that was actually having its closing night! The reality was, not everyone thought it was quite such a rip-roaring success. Mike would tell us later the show had only broken even – which was a worry considering the huge effort that had gone into it and the big turnout.

Future dates were moved to a little later in the year but Mike was unhappy that, in his eyes, I was not promoting the live shows enough. But I could not do it live on *Soccer Saturday* due to broadcasting regulations. I did interviews with regional newspaper after regional newspaper but when Richard Bacon interviewed me on BBC 5 Live, a big football story was breaking and I didn't get the chance to mention the tour. Mike was also frustrated that I would not make a live appearance on *Sunday Brunch*. But my boys, Matt and Robbie, both played football on Sundays and I was their taxi driver/supporter/occasional referee. That was something that was sacrosanct in the Stelling household – I would not miss the boys' games for anything.

The alarm bells should have been ringing but I was still shocked when I got an e-mail from a firm of solicitors informing me that the tour was scrapped and Mike was suing me for breach of contract. Merse and Kammy were both being sued too but not Matt Le Tissier, Thommo or Charlie. A few weeks later, the case was dropped against Kammy. To this day, I have no idea why Mike was so selective.

I hired a solicitor. Our view was that sales figures for future shows were so poor that there could potentially be big financial losses for the organisers and that was the reason the decision had been taken to scrap the tour. I told Sky what was happening. The company has always been very supportive of me, but this time I was a bit disappointed with their reaction, to be frank. They put me in touch with their legal department, but it was made pretty clear that this was my responsibility, not theirs. I understood that to a degree, but much of the official programme that night was produced by the Sky press office (some of whom were there on the opening/closing night). It also carried an advert for Sky Sports and included in those Osman thanked was Andy Melvin, deputy head of Sky Sports!

We felt we had a watertight case. But costs rose and rose. Every e-mail, telephone call, conference call and meeting was followed by a bill. Then we employed a QC and costs rose further and all the while we seemed to get no nearer a resolution. My friends rallied round. My agent Rob Segal (in danger of giving football agents a good name) made a contribution to my costs.

My old boss Vic Wakeling tried to speak to Osman to see if he could help resolve the matter, but to no avail.

The dispute was taking over my life. We were required to provide e-disclosure, allowing the opposite side to go through your e-mails from work and home. When we looked at the e-mails they had to disclose to us in return, we discovered that only 816 seats appeared to have been sold at Wembley a few weeks before the show was due to take place. If 3,000 plus had been at Bournemouth and it had only broken even, then Wembley was going to be a financial disaster.

I remember going out with a group of people to celebrate a friend's birthday. I started to try and explain what was happening but burst into tears and had to leave. It was that bad. My family were being affected by it and focusing on Saturday afternoons was increasingly difficult.

We tried everything to end it. We told Mike we would do two free shows, with him taking the profits. Matt Le Tissier, his friend, tried to speak to him.

With the case set to go to trial, Merse and I agreed to go to mediation. And it was there that I realised why Mike had not accepted any of our offers. He wasn't the one calling the shots. As we gathered round a table at Lambs Chambers in the heart of London's legal-land, there was a face that no-one recognised. He introduced himself as the man who had put his money behind the tour and was determined to get some of it back. Merse and I had never met him before or even heard of him.

After hours of wrangling and getting nowhere at mediation, late in the afternoon he asked to speak to us privately. Against our solicitors' advice we agreed. He put his cards on the table. The gist of it was, 'If this goes to court it could cost the loser £1 million. I can afford to lose a million, can you?' He presented us with an impressive list of the companies and properties he owned – not to mention the helicopter! I had no doubt he had the money. We certainly didn't. There was no way we could win. If Merse and I would do some free shows for him, he would be willing to call a halt to proceedings. It seemed to me we had gone full circle with the only winners being the lawyers, but we accepted the deal.

I went to lunch at the Savoy with him to arrange some dates. Ironically, under other circumstances I felt we would have really liked each other. Several months later, he rang me to say that he had decided he no longer required us to do any shows. He'd had his victory.

It was one of the most stressful periods of my life. It made me wonder how anyone can afford to fight for justice in this country. My solicitor told me, for example, that e-disclosure from the opposition constituted 10,000 pieces of paper. Much of it was irrelevant to the claim, but all of it needed to be reviewed in order, even if only to be discounted. At the going rate that represented a significant amount of my solicitor's time and of course an even more significant amount of my money. It is very hard for the little man to fight and win, no matter how worthy his case.

I have never spoken to Mike Osman since and I doubt I ever will. But I am sure, despite everything, he didn't act through malice. He just got in too deep. And so did we! Safe to say there will never be another *Soccer Saturday Live* tour. I can't afford it.

17

POOLS PASSION

Dear Jeff,

I am a lifelong supporter of Leyton Orient. I along with 406 other members of the Orient family travelled to Crewe on 22 April to see the final meaningful League 2 match for our beloved O's. It was men against boys (we fielded mainly youth players) and the result was never in doubt. I looked to my left at 16.50 and saw the large clock at Crewe count down the final demise of our 112 year league stay. All around me were fans, stunned, shocked, many in tears. We knew it was coming but the reality was like a sledgehammer blow. However I was proud to be an Orient fan as the dignity and behaviour of the deflated O's fans was absolutely exemplary. Although we come from humble East End stock our parents taught us dignity in defeat. What a pity our owner did not have such an upbringing! How can

Bechetti, the owner, not be charged with bringing the game into disrepute? Today Monday 24 April a feeling of utter despondency has surfaced as I think back to people past and present I have had the fortune to call 'Orient family'.

This is not just demotion to non-league – it could be total oblivion. I would ask if you have the chance, please read out my letter to all your viewers to let them know it could happen to their team. Even after three days this feeling is getting worse. Jeff, it is killing me. I can't stop crying while I am writing this letter – Orient are my life.

The raw emotion of a lower league football fan, whose club under terrible ownership stood on the edge of the abyss. Orient survived and returned to the League at the first attempt. But the writer was correct when he said it could happen to other people's clubs. It did. It happened to the club that I had supported since I was a boy.

Hartlepool's Victoria Ground, as it was called then, with its main stand that looked on the verge of collapse, peeling paintwork and prehistoric plumbing was, apart from home, the most important place in my life. It didn't matter that year after year we would be near or at the bottom of the Football League, the players who turned out each week in blue and white stripes were my heroes.

I remember being struck dumb when, delivering football pools coupons one evening, a door was opened by Pools centre-half John Gill. Gill was carved from granite and would happily take ball, player and red card almost simultaneously on a regular basis. He was the darling of the crowd and everything I aspired to.

I had been going to games since I was seven. There had been plenty of hard times. Hartlepool hold the record for the number of times they have been re-elected, the old pals act that in the main kept the league a closed shop in those days. We were often poor and often in financial trouble. Many times I have seen us described as a Cinderella club (fill in your own jokes here). We were the last club in the football league to have floodlights and a temporary wooden stand built in 1916 was still standing in the 1980s. Even relative successes were few and far between. But in my view you don't choose your club. This was the club that did and thankfully still does represent the place of my birth. It will be my club until the day I die, as it will for the many supporters who chant just that every game.

And there have been memorable times. I was already a supporter when Brian Clough and Peter Taylor arrived at the club, taking their first managerial jobs in the Football League. Another great ex-top flight player Cyril Knowles took us to the brink of promotion to what is now League One before tragically passing away with brain cancer. Alan Murray stepped in, finished the job and we went up, but Knowles had done all the ground work and is still a club legend. I was there too when we came within seven minutes of being promoted to the Championship when we led Sheffield Wednesday 2–1 in the play-off final in Cardiff. In the dying minutes, opposition manager Paul Sturrock appeared to be playing a 2–2–6 system with every forward player he had at his disposal on the field as we clung on. With time running out, we conceded a penalty and centre-half Chris Westwood was harshly sent off. Wednesday scored to take the game into extra-time. With ten men, our legs had gone and our hearts were broken as Wednesday won promotion.

If this was harsh on Pools it was even harsher on my friend who had escaped a camping holiday in France with his family by telling his wife early on Saturday morning that he was going for baguettes, but instead drove to the ferry port and arrived in Cardiff ten minutes before kick-off. He returned to his tent in France on Sunday morning, baguettes and flowers in hand. Somehow he remains married.

The thing about supporting a team that rarely has success is that when it does come along, you savour and remember every moment.

Two games after Dave Jones' departure as manager, Hartlepool were relegated from the Football League for the first time in their history. Despite a final-game win over title-chasing Doncaster Rovers, Mark O'Brien's last-minute goal for Newport against Notts County was enough to send us down. On *Soccer Saturday*, I donned my Pools shirt for the final 45 minutes as an act of resistance. It seemed like the end of the world. In fact, things would soon get much worse.

Previous owners Peter Goldberg and Gary Coxall had left the club. John Blackledge and his company Sage Investments had agreed to help the club through a difficult financial period. Eighteen months later, he would pull the plug with the football club owing him £1.8 million. John was unquestionably well intentioned. He had no links with the town, but stepped in to help at the request of Pam Duxbury, the chief finance officer and later chief executive.

On 22 December 2017 John Blackledge put the club up for sale. As well as the money owed to him, Hartlepool United were losing tens of thousands of pounds a week and facing a £200,000 tax bill. Players' wages were not being paid. It was hardly an enticing prospect for any potential buyer. The club were heading towards disaster.

Rachel Cartwright, a local supermarket worker, launched a crowdfunding appeal which brought in a staggering £85,000 to buy a little time. A full house of nearly 7,000 turned out on Save Pools Day as the team played Wrexham – many of them from Middlesbrough in recognition of how Hartlepool helped save their club from going out of business in the 1980s. But when local businessman Chris Musgrave pulled out of negotiations in January, it seemed to be the end of the road. He told me he simply could not work out how much money the club owed or how much he would have to spend to save it. 'I am not prepared to simply sign blank cheques with no end in sight,' he said and who could blame him?

On the spur of the moment, I travelled to Chester for a midweek game convinced I was watching my team for the final time. The memories flooded back for me, especially the FA Cup win over Crystal Palace. Those who go back further than me still talk about the day Pools had come back from 3–0 down to draw level at 3–3 against Manchester United in the FA Cup, only to lose in the final minute. I stood with the fans who were desperate for good news. I had none to give them. I expected the club to go into administration and had been warned that would almost certainly lead to liquidation.

The problem for so many lower league or non-league clubs is that they are almost totally dependent on the benevolence of their owners. Season ticket sales, gate money and the occasional transfer fees are important, but any shortfall usually means the chairman has to put his hand in his pocket. That pocket needs to be deep as running a full-time professional club is not cheap. If only money was distributed more evenly throughout the divisions, clubs further down the pyramid would have more security. Make no mistake, clubs like mine or Chesterfield or Yeovil are the hubs of their communities. Going to a game is the only time four or five thousand people come together with a common interest.

Sometimes fans of Premier League clubs forget how important a nursery non-league can be for the bigger sides. Manchester United's Chris Smalling started at Maidstone, Michail Antonio at Tooting and Mitcham, and Jamie Vardy played for Stocksbridge, Halifax and Fleetwood outside of the Football League. Troy Deeney was at Chelmsley Town. It has always been that way. Ian Wright, Joe Hart and Les Ferdinand all started in non-league football – the list goes on.

Raj Singh was our final hope. He had been in charge of our local rivals Darlington when they had gone into administration and people were sceptical about his reasons for getting involved. Former Pools boss Craig Hignett acted as intermediary and I travelled to the Northeast to meet Raj. He was warm and outgoing and I was immediately impressed. He outlined how much he would be willing to put in. But he wanted fellow investors. Despite dozens of phone calls and e-mails, promises from America and Sweden proved hollow. I agreed to help. Raj would put in well over £1 million over four years (in fact he ended up putting in around £2 million in the first couple of years). I would put in a six-figure sum as a one-off. I badgered my contacts at Sky Bet who agreed to a £50,000 ground-naming rights deal.

But the challenges were immense. Players were on two-year contracts worth up to £70,000-a-man in salaries, way above the normal rate of most players at the fifth tier of English football. There was a claim against the club for a six-figure sum from one-time part-owner Peter Goldberg. A laundry refused to return the team kit because they hadn't been paid. Things were so bad that before the takeover deal could go through, Pam Duxbury rang Raj to say the club would be unable to stage a home game as they could not afford to pay for stewarding and emergency services. Raj advanced them £15,000 of his own money to make sure the game went ahead and stave off the threat of points being docked. The game went ahead – but there were no chips on sale at the ground. We could not afford the electricity.

And we could not afford £1.8 million for John Black-ledge. He had told me many times that his only interest was ensuring the club survived and I believed him. But with a deadline for completion of the deal just two days away, there had been no agreement. The newspapers reported this as a snag and it was – a £1.8 million snag. At the eleventh hour, John came good. He agreed to getting his money back in a series of sliding-scale payments, dependent on which division the club were playing in. Before the final game of the season, a 2–1 win away at Tranmere on 28 April, Raj and I were officially named as the new owners of the club.

A busy summer followed. Contracts needed renegotiating at reduced salaries. Some players agreed, some refused and left. The club bought out the contracts of others that we didn't need but who still had a year guaranteed – short-term pain for long-term gain. We brought in a new chief executive, rebranded the ground 'The Super Six Stadium' and made sure chips were back on the menu.

Prior to the first home game of the following season against Harrogate, the new chairman and I were asked to go onto the pitch. Nearly 4,000 fans had turned up. They chanted *'Raj and Jeff's blue and white army'*. It was one of the best feelings of my life.

18

PREMATURELY RETIRED

It was at about half-past-eight in the morning in March 2017 when the phone next to my hotel bed rang. A talk-SPORT radio producer wanted me to be interviewed on *Alan Brazil Sports Breakfast* to chat about my impending retirement. Talk about a wake-up call! I'm not ready for the full-time whistle to be blown on my career just yet, though I accept I may have taken the occasional glance at the added-time board.

I have been at Sky more than a quarter of a century. A couple of years ago I got an e-mail telling me so, and that I would be receiving a commemorative plaque and could choose a gift from the company to mark the occasion. The internal web ite with the gift selection appeared to be down, so I rang the number for enquiries. A stern sounding lady told me that I would not have completed 25 years at Sky until the following day and so couldn't pick my gift until then!

It is fair to say that when I was quizzed at my senior school by the Dickensian-style headmaster – black cape, translucent skin, rimless glasses perched on sharp nose, cane always in hand – I couldn't have anticipated that I would be in the business for so long.

'Journalism is no sort of a career for a boy from this school, Stelling. Are you a snoop? Do you enjoy prying into people's private lives?' he demanded. In fact, he was making it sound quite appealing.

The *Sun* featured me in a list of the longest serving broadcasters in British TV – and that was in 2013!

But I was bemused by the telephone call from talk-SPORT. I told them that I had no intention of hanging up the mic and then immediately phoned Barney Francis, MD of Sky Sports, to find out if he knew something that I didn't and to reassure him it was fake news. In fact that morning's Ooh-aah *Daily Star* had the headline '**Sky Sports Legend to retire after more than 40 years**' emblazoned across one of its inside pages and had the quotes to back it up.

'Sky Sports legend Jeff Stelling, 62, last night revealed he is dreaming of relaxing in the sunshine.

'He told the *Daily Star*: "I don't know how much longer I will do presenting. I have done it for 40 years. I might want to put my feet up. I am getting on. The next decision will be about retirement."

'The dad of three wants to relax in Portugal with his family. "I want to stick my feet up on the beach. We spend as much time as possible in Portugal when it is not the football season. I love it there. I would be happy to spend more time there."

'They even quoted bookies' odds for who was most likely to take over from me. The runners and riders included:

David Jones 11/10 fav
Julian Warren 6/4
Simon Thomas 2/1
Natalie Sawyer 3/1
Rachel Riley 5/1
Adrian Chiles 50/1
Piers Morgan 100/1
Chris Kamara 200/1

It soon dawned on me what had happened. Weeks earlier I had spoken to the *Daily Star* about my plans for 15 marathons in 15 days later in the summer. I hadn't spoken to the *Star* since. This story was clearly from things I had said to the reporter then, re-hashed and definitely misinterpreted.

The quotes were probably accurate, but they were answers to different questions. The reporter had asked about my TV ambitions, to which I responded something on the lines of 'Ambitions? I've presented for 40 years. My ambition is to put my feet up in the sun in Portugal. The next decision I will have to make is about retirement.' I do like the idea of spending time putting my feet up in Portugal, but not permanently and not now.

The cobbled together retirement story was nonsense, but people still ask me about it now. After all, it was there in black and white and not just in the *Daily Star*. The *Independent* ran the same story pretty much word for word without bothering to ask me about it. Whatever happened to journalism?

The story didn't worry me too much, in truth. Some of the reactions were actually very flattering.

Dear Jeff,

I have just read about your impending retirement and had to write to you. We watch Soccer Saturday from start to finish together every week and have done for years. Sometimes we watch it rather than go to a game. (We are all Sunderland fans so it is an easy choice.) My boys have grown up watching you. They call you Uncle Jeff. What are we going to do if you retire? Please don't retire Jeff. We all love you. Please, please, please, please, please, please, please carry on.

With love

Dorothy Johnstone

Twitter was awash with it.

> @nd_yaho: No Jeff ur not allowed to retire. Want my kids to enjoy Soccer Saturday.

> @neiljohn1807: Unbelievable Jeff.

> @DevamMUFC: Nooooooooooooooooooooooooooo.

> @BVF_Mike: Is this some sort of sick joke?

> @olivermann100: F*** no!

> @stumplus: He can broadcast from Portugal . . . sorted.

> @seannyybt: Jeff should be immortal. Everyone needs to witness him at some point in their life.

> @philthompson: Thank Christ for that.

> @chris_kammy: I can reassure everyone that it will be a very long time before Unbelievable Jeff will be retiring.

Of course retirement comes to everyone – though sometimes too soon. I am still disappointed that the doyen of sports broadcasting, cool, unflappable, entertaining Des Lynam disappeared from our screens far too early. In the last few years, a lot of the people I have worked with have decided to step down. Eddie Hemmings and

Mike Stevenson from Rugby League, David Livingstone after 26 years hosting the golf coverage, Ian Condron the long-time *Soccer Saturday* producer and good friend, and Martin Turner, the brilliant mastermind behind Sky's Formula One and darts coverage, are no longer in and around the studios.

Of course the doyen of darts commentary, Sid 'Even Hypotenuse would have had trouble working out these angles' Waddell, died in 2012.

And my old boss, friend, mentor and protector Vic Wakeling sadly passed away aged 73. It is no reflection on the people who have replaced them, but the Sky Sports studios are not quite the same for me. Sky is a young and vibrant company and from time to time I admit I do feel a bit of a dinosaur. Then I catch sight of Martin Tyler and feel a little less so. Martin is nine years older than me and as outstanding and authoritative a football commentator as ever. I tell myself if Martin is still going strong, then I can too. After all, Bruce Forsyth carried on deep into his eighties and David Attenborough is still going strong in his nineties. I might have another 20 years or more to go.

The 2019–20 season had already been a tricky one for me before coronavirus brought it to a premature halt. In my time at Sky, I had only ever missed two Saturday programmes when there was a full football fixture list, one through illness and one when my son Matt was born. Conveniently he was delivered just before the start of *Match of the Day*. But this season I had already taken three Saturdays off work for a hand operation. I suffer from a condition known as Dupuytrens Contracture which can prevent the straightening of fingers. The surgeon told me that it is most prevalent in those descended from Vikings. When a genealogy company had traced my family tree a few years earlier, they decided I was either from a family of Northumbrian pig farmers or from Viking stock. Here was confirmation of what I had always known! Maybe missing those shows had also fuelled the speculation that I was ready to step down.

I have never been under any sort of pressure to give up. In fact, Sky Sports' new MD, Rob Webster, told me in his first meeting with me that I can carry on presenting *Soccer Saturday* for as long as I wish. Having had a taste of what retirement might be like during the coronavirus crisis where I was sidelined for goodness knows how long, I can tell Rob I don't plan calling it a day just yet.

And even though the SJA awards may have dried up, there's still a regular trickle from elsewhere. In my office, there are three Sports Presenter of the Year awards from 2012 to 2017 from the Television and Radio Industry Club. There should be four in all honesty, but after a night of overexuberant celebration I left the fourth on a South Western Railway train bound for Poole. I asked about it at lost property but with no success. Presumably, someone is sitting at home in Poole with a Jeff Stelling Sports Presenter of the Year award on their mantelpiece.

I received an honorary degree in Professional Studies from Teesside University, though ironically and very unprofessionally I almost nodded off during the ceremony.

In 2010, I was awarded the Freedom of Hartlepool, which means I can now drive my sheep through the town. I suspect that the mayor, Stuart Drummond, had more than a hand in it. Stuart was H'Angus the Monkey, the Hartlepool United mascot when he first stood for mayor in 2002 with the campaigning slogan 'Free Bananas for all Children'. Two days before polling day, his election agent told me, 'We could cause a real shock here. We could come second.' Of course he won, and after resisting calls for him to stand down – he was working full time in a call centre – he went on to be re-elected in 2005 and again in 2009.

I'm lucky enough to have been to Olympic Games, World Cups, World Athletics Championships, Champions League finals, World Darts finals and Grand Nationals. Just at Sky I have presented Football, Darts, Snooker, Horse Racing, Pool, Cricket, Rugby League,

Greyhound Racing, Angling, Golf and Boxing as well as *Soccer Saturday*. I have met so many brilliant people from all of those sports and the years have simply flown past.

To be honest, the hardest thing about the job has been growing old in public view. Every year more grey hair, more inches on the waist, less good eyesight. You fight it the best way you can – a touch of hair colour, one less beer, contact lenses and perhaps the odd spot of Botox – but it is always going to be a losing contest. Admitting to Botox doesn't concern me, but on one occasion within seconds of arriving at the Harley Street clinic, a young woman, sunglasses on, collar up, hat pulled low, looking every inch an Eastern European spy made a hasty exit. A few moments later, her name was called. She was a *Sky Sports News* presenter who clearly did not want me to know that she was getting a little help in the age war. Before you jump to any conclusions, it was not Bianca Westwood! Just as well, as my Botox doc Nick Milojevic is a massive Arsenal fan. Goodness knows what would happen to a West Ham fan under his treatment. He is also the best in the business and has a sprinkling of celebrities on his books. He once told me he had given Botox to one of the female members of the *Made in Chelsea* cast. I have watched religiously to try and work out which one, but it is impossible. It is a wrinkle-free programme!

A letter I got in February 2020 was addressed to 'Jeff Stirling, Sky Sports Football, somewhere in London, or England,' so I feel I still have work to do in establishing myself.

But I am certain I will know when my time is finally up. When David Wagner was appointed manager at Huddersfield Town, I assumed that being from Frankfurt he should be called 'Vagner'.

'No,' said Merse. 'It's Wagner. His dad was American.'

Corrected by Paul Merson on pronunciation. If that ever happens again, I'm done.

19

LIKE IT OR NOT

A lot has changed at Sky since I first darkened their doors in the mid-1990s. The Portakabins that were once the studies are long gone. So too have all the other businesses that used to be the neighbours. Now Sky is a small city in itself. Studios and offices are interspersed with a choice of restaurants, a cinema, a supermarket, a hairdressers and a gym. At Christmas, an ice rink is installed. There were plans to add a swimming pool but that was put on hold. Just as well. I wouldn't want to put anyone through the trauma of witnessing me in Speedos!

A lot has changed in football too since *Soccer Saturday* reporter Dickie Davies asked Rio Ferdinand, then at West Ham, if he could do an 'at home' piece with the England defender.

'No problem,' replied Rio, 'but I will have to follow you Dickie because I don't know where you live!'

Needless to say I have views on some of these changes. Now these are not rants but . . .

MEDIA ACCESS TO PLAYERS

These days Dickie would not have been allowed even to ask Rio for an interview. Those requests go through club press officers who rule with the sort of iron grip that Dominic Cummings shows with the Conservatives. Some of them, though not all, believe they should be a barrier to prevent access for the media to players rather than facilitate it. It is not just TV and radio. I used to love building up to the weekend's big games by reading the Saturday newspapers. Now pick up any one of them and you will see the same features in all of them. The Premier League and the clubs provide an interviewee and everyone dutifully covers the press conference. Half the time the players offered up are fringe players or poor English speakers. Gone are the days when a journalist's contacts book could earn him a nice exclusive. It was much easier in my younger days. I would turn up at Ayresome Park every other day and ask whichever Middlesbrough player was around – Graeme Souness, David Armstrong, Willie Maddren, David Hodgson, Terry Cooper, Bozo Jankovic – and it was up to them if they were happy to be interviewed. Even though they were top-flight players, most were keen to help.

At Sky, I remember Peter Crouch doing a feature for *Soccer Saturday* which involved him sticking his neck out of the skylight at his home (no, I have no idea why!) and Robbie Savage giving Tony Cottee a tour of his lavish home and cars. Johnny Phillips went to visit the Watford goalkeeper Richard Lee at his hat shop. I went to interview Steven Gerrard at his Liverpool bar. Now every interview is done at the training ground or in a featureless room under the watchful eye of a club official.

I remember suggesting that we should try and get Danny Ings to revisit some of the places where he had grown up on his return to Southampton for a *Soccer Saturday* feature. I doubt the request ever got to him. We ended up interviewing him on the training ground.

Pre-match interviews on the day are now are restricted to three questions which have to be about the game. It means bland 'How do you see it going?' and 'How much are you looking forward to it?' types of question. I nag the *Soccer Saturday* producers not to use them. If anyone is going to bore the pants off the viewers, it may as well be me.

In my view, fans would relate much better to players if they knew what they were really like. People say there aren't any characters in the game anymore. I think they are wrong. There are plenty of players with loads of character. They're just not allowed to show it.

VAR

I suspected we were heading for chaos when former Premier League referee Neil Swarbrick explained at a pre-season seminar for the media that under VAR, two identical fouls happening simultaneously at different games could result in two different rulings, but both would be correct. Sounds bonkers? It is, as I quickly pointed out to Neil. The PGMOL, the Professional Game Match Officials Board, wants to support the on-field referee in their judgements. So if one ref thought a challenge was a red card offence while another thought an identical challenge was just a foul, the VAR would support both of them.

'You do realise that is leaving VAR open to total ridicule,' I told Neil.

Of course, by now the PGMOL should be well used to ridicule. Despite the fact that VAR was being operated in Europe, they had decided to do it their own way and never consult the pitchside monitors. I could have got a handy price for all those lovely unused televisions that have spent the past season sitting untouched on the touchline.

The mantra is always that a referee would only be overruled if there was a clear and obvious error, but that doesn't happen most of the time either. It was the failure of VAR to award a penalty to Leicester against Arsenal for the clearest foul you would ever see by Matteo Guendouzi on Caglar Soyuncu in November 2019 that finally made me erupt.

'Scrap it, scrap VAR, scrap it now, scrap it this weekend over the international break because it is worthless, pointless, a total waste of time. Please Mike Riley, come and tell us how that is not a penalty. Come and tell us because we can't understand. These four guys [panellists], they played football for a living, and they cannot understand. Come and enlighten us because we are not seeing the vision at the moment.'

Needless to say we are still waiting to be enlightened. I was a supporter of VAR because there are so many refereeing errors that are easy to spot with the benefit of a closer look. But can anybody honestly tell me the game in England is better for VAR in its current form?

And if I wanted offside decisions to be decided using set squares, compasses and protractors – or the digital equivalents of them – I would have let my old maths teachers referee games.

UNDER-21 TEAMS IN EFL TROPHY

Here are the football results:

Burton Albion 0 Middlesbrough U-21s 1
Grimsby Town 1 Leicester City U-21s 2
Stevenage 1 Fulham U-21s 1

If you missed those games don't worry, so did most people. They attracted less than a thousand fans – between them. The lowest at Burton's Pirelli Stadium was watched by 202. I have seen more at a Sunday League game. This is the EFL trophy where academy sides are invited to take part against League clubs. In a crowded football calendar, these are games that no-one needs or wants to watch. It is true that the final at Wembley does get a good attendance, though that would not be the case if an Under-21 side reached it. Chelsea's kids had the good grace to lose in the semi-final a couple of years ago.

The elite team's academy coaches will doubtless point to the fact that it gives their youngsters good play-ing time against experienced, full-time professionals. Yet ironically, league clubs playing their youngsters against the Under-21s have been fined for playing weakened teams! In fact the rules were tightened a couple of years ago to make punishments even tougher. If top-level clubs really want their kids to get experience of something other than Under-21s football, send them on loan to a lower league or national league side. Yet many are reluctant to do that. I remember many years ago talking to Danny Welbeck, then at Manchester United, and Victor Anichebe of Everton. Welbeck had been sent out on loan twice and he felt his career had flourished partly due to that. Anichebe had stayed at Everton playing in youth and reserve teams and felt he had suffered because of it.

And a late result:

Gillingham 0 Tottenham U-21s 4 – attendance 304

EXPECTED GOALS

Hartlepool fans rarely expect goals, not for us anyway, so perhaps that's why it has taken me a long time to get to grips with the expected goals statistic that features on *Match of the Day*.

Expected goals is in theory an aid to football betting that assesses the chance of a shot being a goal based on the quality and quantity of shots to prove that some scorelines can be misleading. An example often given is a game that finished Arsenal 1 Stoke 1 but expected goals was Arsenal 1.41, Stoke 0.69. But you don't need expected goals to know that Stoke took a battering – just watch the highlights or read the reports. I probably am a dinosaur but I simply do not get it. In February 2020, just before coronavirus stopped play, *FourFourTwo* magazine revealed how the Premier League table would look under expected goals. Newcastle United were bottom, West Ham second bottom and Norwich eighteenth.

That tells me that if you are a punter using expected goals as your mantra, expected losses will soon follow.

EUROPA LEAGUE

Here's a quiz for you. What do F91 Dudelange, FC Olexandria, Skenderbeu Korce, Fastav Zlin, MOL Vidi and Vorskla Poltava have in common? The answer – in recent seasons they have all qualified to play in the group phase of the Europa League. In England, some clubs spend an entire season trying to qualify to compete against sides like the ones I have just listed. Then they spend the next season wondering why they bothered. It is disruptive to their domestic campaigns and expensive to reach far-flung destinations. Even worse, if your team manages to navigate its way past Akhisarspor and Jablonec in the group stages, they then face the possibility of having to play a side which has just dropped out of the Champions League like Inter Milan or Napoli. This is a seriously flawed tournament.

HALF-AND-HALF SCARVES

Unthinkable. Unacceptable. Unwearable. Manchester United/Liverpool – you cannot be serious! I know we all want football to be less tribal but no football fan over the age of 10 would contemplate wearing one. Try putting on a half-and-half scarf when Boca Juniors play River Plate!

SHIRTS

Poor dads. Once it was just your club's first-team kit that made the ideal gift for your child. Then away kits were introduced, which I understand and accept due to the potential for colour clashes. But what possible excuse can there be for a third kit other than to cynically manipulate fans into spending yet more of their hard-earned cash on a shirt that will rarely be worn and never be needed? Fans pay enough for season tickets, programmes, price-inflated food and drink and transport. If a club's away kit is a clash with the opposition colours, then simply revert to the home strip. A third shirt is redundant. It is just a rip-off and clubs should be ashamed.

THE FA CUP

If the FA Cup is ever to regain its gloss – and I doubt it ever will, to be truthful – the televised games can't be allowed to stretch from the Friday night deep into the following week. I know the smaller clubs are desperate for the financial rewards of having their games televised but many games now are also switched to Sunday, so that often Saturdays feature a handful of matches, usually those with the least appeal. I remember when 3 o'clock on third round day in the FA Cup was the start of one of the most exciting afternoons of the season. Wrexham's win over Arsenal in 1992 was on a Saturday, as was Bradford's famous win at Stamford Bridge against Chelsea, Barnsley's win at Liverpool and Shrewsbury's win over Everton in 2003. There's little or no chance that those ties would now be played on a Saturday. My view is let TV pick their matches for Friday, Saturday, Sunday and Monday and insist that every other tie kicks off at 3 o'clock on a Saturday afternoon.

I also believe the FA Cup should be seeded so that the 20 lower league and non-league sides who have battled their way through to the third round are guaranteed a game against a team from the top two divisions. It will mean bigger paydays for some of the smaller clubs and more potential giant-killings. Last season Hartlepool won their qualifying round game and then had to overcome trips to Yeovil and Torquay. Our reward was an away game at League One Oxford!

BOOKINGS FOR REMOVING SHIRTS

The single most stupid law in the game. The governing body insists it incites fans when a player removes his shirt after scoring and I understand that could be the case if it is done in front of opposition supporters. But this is a mandatory punishment. If a player tears his shirt off in the emotion of scoring a last-minute winning goal and celebrates with his own team-mates and fans, why should he be punished? Where do we draw the line? Couldn't every form of celebration be seen as incitement? At times we forget football is meant to be entertainment.

It can also put referees in difficult positions. When Demarai Gray removed his shirt after scoring for Leicester in the aftermath of the tragic helicopter crash outside the King Power Stadium that killed everyone on board, ref Lee Probert was duty-bound to produce a yellow card. The fact that the player's undershirt carried the words 'For Khun Vichai' in tribute to the club owner who had perished, made no difference. He had to stick to the letter of this ludicrous, unwanted law.

E-GAMERS

I arrived at Sky one Saturday morning to find the reception area awash with young men. A FIFA e-Tournament was being held on the premises. Not wanting to be the grumpy, out-of-touch old fogey (keep your opinions to yourself please), I asked one person, his red tracksuit top emblazoned with sponsors' names, if he was playing. He told me he wasn't a player, he was a coach. I asked him if the kit man and physio had gone on ahead! Seriously enjoy the game guys, but remember you are not footballers and this is not a sport.

STEREOTYPES

I hate the fact that all footballers seem to be categorised as young men who have too much, too soon and don't know what to do with it. The stereotype was even more prominent during the coronavirus crisis. We read in lurid headlines about Manchester City's Kyle Walker hosting a party of sorts, Oumar Niasse of Everton being stopped by police while out with friends in his £100,000 Mercedes and there was story after story about players rejecting pay cuts. But the truth is that they are a soft target. I am happy to say that most of the people I have met in the game over the years have been perfectly nice – though that would rarely be reported. When my kids were small and a handful, people like Aidy Boothroyd, Stiliyan Petrov and Michael Brown would splash around with them when we bumped into them on holiday. No-one from any profession is more approachable than Peter Crouch. When I bumped into Preston's Scott Sinclair on holiday in Dubai he was charming and gracious. Crystal Palace manager Roy Hodgson is generous with his time when people spot him, as is former manager Alan Pardew.

One story that did make the press was when Watford keeper Ben Foster spotted an elderly man in a ditch by a dual carriageway as he drove home from a match. Foster turned his car around, took the man home, helped clean him up and later asked him to join them for Christmas dinner. Like Foster most footballers are intrinsically decent people. Just don't wait until they are about to take their first mouthful of dinner before you go and ask for a selfie.

SPORTS SCIENCE

A few years ago a Premier League player told how a sports scientist at his club had said to him: 'I don't think you should train today. Take a rest day.' A couple of seasons ago I was surprised that Nicky Featherstone, one of Hartlepool's best players, wasn't starting a winnable game. I was told that the club's sports scientists had decided that if he continued to start every game, he was not going to be at his peak for the Christmas programme, several weeks away. I don't doubt that sports scientists have an important role to play at clubs, but let's leave picking the team to the manager or coach.

EUROPEAN CHAMPIONSHIP 2020

I know it didn't happen due to coronavirus, but the idea of playing the Euros in a host of different venues is madness. What next – the World Cup played across five continents? Football's authorities have already shown that they don't care a jot about the fans by deciding to stage games as far apart as Baku, Bucharest, St Petersburg and Dublin. I am fortunate to have been to major football tournaments and they are festivals. Of course the games are important, but so is the experience of mingling with fans from different nations, drinking in the atmosphere and the alcohol (in moderation), having an experience that will stay with them for the rest of their lives. This format means it is near impossible to get to matches and ridiculously expensive. Perhaps the only good thing to come out of the Covid-19 crisis is that UEFA and the rest realise how crucial fans are to the game.

Just in case you think I am a grumpy old man, there have been changes that I like.

STADIUMS

Football stadiums, from the grandest to the most modest have improved immeasurably. In the past only the poshest parts of the ground had seats or even roofs. Food was non-existent, Bovril was the only drink available and the toilets were liable to leave you scarred for life. As a child the toilet facilities at Hartlepool consisted of a square of corrugated iron with no roof and no real drainage. If you needed more than a pee, then good luck! As far as I am aware there was nowhere in the standing area of the ground where you could do that. I am not a member of the prawn sandwich brigade but it is nice that you can now sit in comfort at grounds, stay dry, and get a bite to eat and drink. My two sons, aged 21 and 20, tell me they have never tasted Bovril. Now that is an indication of how much the game has changed for the better.

FAMILIES

It is great now that you can go to games as a family. I remember in the 1970s and '80s how threatening it was to go to a match. You could forget about a drink in a local pub pre-match – that just was not possible. Visiting fans would be constantly in danger, especially when leaving a ground to get to a train or tube station. That walk could be daunting even for a neutral. I remember as a BBC radio reporter often feeling very uncomfortable effectively running the gauntlet of National Front supporters as I walked from the underground station to Upton Park or vice versa. Not everything is perfect nowadays and there are games that I would not take a young family to, but mostly things have improved hugely.

NATIONS LEAGUE

I admit I thought this was a tournament too many when it was first announced. But I was wrong. It gets rid of so many meaningless friendlies and gives teams like England the chance to play top-quality opposition. England produced their best 45 minutes under Gareth Southgate in Seville when racing into a 3–0 lead over Spain. It was a fantastic match and England went on to reach the last four. I think it is here to stay and will grow in significance.

FANCY DRESS

It is great to see fans produce a party atmosphere to the end of seasons by going to games in fancy dress. Hundreds of Hartlepool fans dressed as penguins on London tube trains, escalators and in pubs en route to Crawley is a memory I will take with me to my grave. They went to Charlton as Smurfs and on a second visit, Oompa-Loompas, to Plymouth as Stormtroopers, to Cheltenham as mime artists, to Tranmere as clowns, to Barrow as knights and to Carlisle as Bob Marleys. Long may it continue.

There is one thing I would like to see in football:

TIMEKEEPERS

How often is three minutes the amount of time added in football matches? Time and again referees seem to be unaware of how much time has been lost during the course of a game. I think, as it is in many sports, this should be taken out of the referee's hands. After all, would you expect a boxing ref to be timing each three minutes? Of course not. So let's allow the men in the middle to concentrate on the game and have an independent timekeeper during matches.

And the following one to mull over:

TIES OR NOT

A season or so ago, there was a *Soccer Saturday* revolution. Wearing ties was banned. There was an outcry among the watching public, or at least my wife. The counter revolution was led by Phil Thompson who defiantly put his back on, clearly realising it was going to take more than the removal of a tie to modernise him! The ties were back. But now they are off on *Sky Sports*

News. I am not sure I like it. I would not expect to see Mark Austin or Huw Edwards present the national news without neckwear, so should we expect to see Julian Waters or Mike Wedderburn without theirs? Perhaps they should do what they often do. Run a poll.

20

THANKS

Dear Jeff and the boys,

Thank you for the best day of my life! I had an amazing time and I learned so many things about being a sports presenter and reporting on football games. Come on Ipswich!

From

George

George had come into the Sky Sports studio one Saturday, sat down, loved it and stayed as long as he could.

Which is rather like what I have done. I could not have anticipated when I got the bus to the office of the *Hartlepool Mail* in 1973, without a driving licence or shorthand or much of a clue, or when I spoke my first words on radio four years later, that it would all have worked out so well.

So to Sky Sports and all the other broadcasters who have employed me, thanks for the best days of my life.

And thank you for watching me, listening to me and now reading about me as I learned about being a sports presenter and hopefully put those lessons into practice.

But enough of this. There's been a goal at Hartlepool, but which way has it gone . . . ?

Acknowledgements

With thanks to:

Rob and Emma, my agents.

Jonathan Taylor at Headline for his encouragement and persistence.

Lizzie, Robbie, Matt and Olivia for listening to extracts time and time and time again without complaint.

Postman Michael for delivering my letters, even if there were some I didn't want.

Gilbert the ginger cat for moving from his preferred position on the PC keyboard for long enough to allow me to complete this book.

Index